21 *(Surprisingly Simple)*
STEPS *to a* GREAT LIFE

Tyndale House Publishers, Inc., Wheaton, Illinois

Surprisingly Simple

21 STEPS

to a GREAT

LIFE

DR. STEVE STEPHENS

Visit Tyndale's exciting Web site at www.tyndale.com

TYNDALE is a registered trademark of Tyndale House Publishers, Inc.

Tyndale's quill logo is a trademark of Tyndale House Publishers, Inc.

Designed by Jessie McGrath

Library of Congress Cataloging-in-Publication Data

Stephens, Steve.
   21 (surprisingly simple) steps to a great life / Steve Stephens.
     p. cm.
   Includes bibliographical references.
   ISBN 1-4143-0174-X (pbk.)
   1. Christian life—Baptist authors.   I. Title: Twenty one (surprisingly simple) steps to a great life. II. Title.
   BV4501.3.S745 2005
   248.4—dc22
                                       2004027403

Printed in United States of America

10 09 08 07 06 05
7   6   5   4   3   2   1

DEDICATION

To all those who have passed their wisdom on to me and to others

FREE DISCUSSION GUIDE!

A discussion guide for
21 (Surprisingly Simple) Steps to a Great Life
is available at

Christianbookguides.com

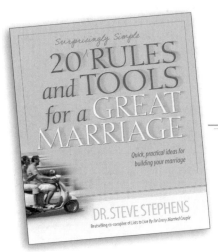

**ALSO AVAILABLE BY
DR. STEVE STEPHENS**

ISBN: 0-8423-6203-7 $9.99

If you want a marriage that's simply great, keep it simple!

Having a great marriage isn't necessarily complex. It's about the basics.

With clear, to-the-point principles, Dr. Steve Stephens provides practical ways to keep your marriage strong and vibrant. Each chapter includes a prayer for strengthening your marriage and concrete ideas for helping you and your spouse enjoy each other as never before.

You'll be surprised at how applying a few simple rules can make a good marriage better . . . or keep a struggling marriage from falling apart. So learn the rules—and look forward to a relationship that's simply great.

CONTENTS

ACKNOWLEDGMENTS

Few projects are completed in a void. Even when a project is shouldered primarily by one person, many others come along to bring that project from concept to reality. This book is no exception.

First and foremost is my wife. Tami is constantly there with her love and encouragement.

Then there are my three children, who tolerate my writing when they'd rather be playing. Brittany, Dylan, and Dusty are great kids who I pray will have truly great lives.

I thank my parents for always being there with a smile and a positive word. I also thank Tami's parents for their typing and proofreading of this manuscript.

A few of the others who helped bring this book to the readers include: John VanDiest and John Shepherd for their feedback on my initial ideas; Jan Long Harris for taking the risk to present this idea to Tyndale and championing the concept; Lisa Jackson for her enthusiasm, practical insights, and excellent editing; the entire Tyndale family, from the cover designers to the marketing department; Keeley Hannon, my office manager and cheerleader, who faithfully structures my schedule and keeps track of hundreds of loose ends; and the New Vision Class at Milwaukie Baptist Church, who let me test out much of this material on them.

God bless you all, and live wisely.

Dr. Steve Stephens

INTRODUCTION
SEEK WISDOM

Why do people do the things they do?

I ask myself this question at least ten times a day—and that's on a good day. How can good, smart, capable people do such foolish things? What perplexes me even more is why these same people continue to repeat their own self-sabotaging behavior year after year. Don't they realize what they're doing? Don't they want to stop? Many of those I speak to know that something is wrong. As a popular songwriter recently put it: "I'm a train wreck waiting to happen." The dilemma is that they don't know what to do about it.

Too many people are living less-than-fulfilled lives. Their lives may not be disasters, but they don't have the excitement, joy, or a sense of purpose. Wise people have a fulfilled life. They live each day intentionally and have discovered that wisdom is satisfying and incredibly powerful.

As I have counseled people over the past twenty-five years, I have observed that many have lost touch with the concept of wisdom. In our fast-paced, multitasked, sound-bite culture, wisdom is thought of as old-fashioned, boring, and irrelevant. Yet nothing could be further from the truth. Wisdom is exciting, life-changing, and incredibly inspirational. As Solomon, king of Israel and one of the wisest men in history, wrote: "Blessed is the man who finds wisdom, . . . for she is more profitable than silver and yields better returns than gold. . . . Long life is in her right hand; in her left hand are riches and honor. Her ways are pleasant ways, and all her paths are peace."[1]

We need wisdom. John Patrick wrote that "wisdom makes life endurable." It also makes life meaningful, impactful, and, ultimately, deeply satisfying. Yet there is another aspect to wisdom: It protects us from harm, guards us from foolishness, and sets us on a track to health (mentally, emotionally, physically, socially, and spiritually). Without wisdom we are poised for self-destruction. In his book *The Best Question Ever*, Andy Stanley writes that the most important question in life is, "What is the wise thing to do?" By asking this question we start to reshape our lives. We avoid the parallel questions that have gotten us into so much trouble:

- What is easy?

- What is exciting?

- What is fun?

- What is financially beneficial?

- What is safe?

- What is acceptable?

- What is politically correct?

- What is impressive?

- What is personally satisfying?

- What is professionally advantageous?

These are not necessarily bad questions, but they aren't the most important one.

I want to be a seeker of wisdom. I have seen the consequences of those who have not found wisdom, and their lives bear multiple scars. Solomon continued his writing on wisdom: "Leave your simple ways behind, and begin to live; learn to use good judgment. . . . If you scorn wisdom, you will be the one to suffer."[2] I do not claim to be wise, but I wish to look faithfully for wisdom and embrace it whenever I stumble upon it. Yet wisdom is not just a matter of chance. James wrote that "if you need wisdom, . . . ask God, and he will give it to you."[3] Wisdom is not beyond your reach, shrouded in some esoteric form or hidden in something beyond your comprehension. Yet wisdom is not always as obvious as I'd like it to be.

We live in a culture of knowledge, and we frequently confuse knowledge with wisdom. Michel Quoist wrote: "Knowledgeable people are found everywhere, but we are cruelly short of wise people." We collect knowledge but often spurn wisdom. Charles Spurgeon taught that "wisdom is the right use of knowledge." In fact, I would go on to say that knowledge without wisdom can be very dangerous. But knowledge *with* wisdom can be the most valuable gift you have ever received.

This is a book of wisdom. I say that with no pride or arrogance, for none of what I write is new or unique. The wisdom here is universal, collected from many people on many continents over many centuries. I am simply a weaver who has placed these strands of truth and wisdom into a loom and worked them into a piece of cloth. The strands include stories, conversations, quotations, observations, Scripture passages, and personal experience. There is much missing, for it is but one small piece of cloth. As I think of all the strands of wisdom I do not yet understand, I am reminded of Sir Isaac Newton's words: "Here I stand on the edge of an ocean of truth. I have picked up a few grains of sand, but the whole ocean lies before me unknown."

So now is the time to start a journey into twenty-one essentials of wisdom. Each of the following chapters will highlight one important aspect of a life characterized by wisdom. As you seek wisdom, you will be amazed at how your life begins to change. Wisdom is the currency of a good and satisfying life. Understanding these principles will make you rich, much richer than you ever imagined. Reading is easy, but you might find many excuses for not applying what you have read. Knowing and doing are two totally different tasks. In spite of our complaints and discontent about how things are, we have grown familiar and comfortable with our situation. This makes us lazy and resistant to change. Yet wisdom frequently insists upon change, for it is through change that we stretch, grow, and mature. Wisdom is active. A wise person walks the high road and avoids the ways of foolishness. It may not be popular or easy, but wisdom is a good thing, and its rewards are many. Those who disregard wisdom will only end in regret.

In his book *The Great Divorce*, C. S. Lewis writes about a man with a red lizard on his shoulder. This wicked animal was sucking the life out of the man, so an angel appeared to help him remove this horrible lizard. Yet the man had grown used to his situation, and the very thought of losing his lizard seemed too drastic. But the angel was persistent about the need to do something and do it now.

"Look! It's gone to sleep of its own accord. I'm sure it'll be all right now. Thanks ever so much."

"May I kill it?"

"Honestly, I don't think there's the slightest necessity for that. I'm sure I shall be able to keep it in order now. I think a more gradual process would be far better than killing it."

"The gradual process is of no use at all," said the angel.

". . . I'll think over what you've said very carefully. I honestly will. . . . But as a matter of fact I'm not feeling frightfully well to-day. It would be most silly to do it now. . . . Some other day, perhaps."

If something is wise, then to delay using that wisdom doesn't make sense. It is foolish. Unused wisdom does nobody any good. If you know what to do, why don't you do it? So once you recognize wisdom, step up and apply it. Don't hesitate, but do it right now. Joshua, the leader who guided the Israelites into the Promised Land, said, "Be strong and courageous! . . . For the LORD your God is with you wherever you go."[4] Don't allow your fear or discomfort to hold you back. Instead, get excited and embrace wisdom. I love the following words by Annie Besant: "Never forget that life can only be nobly inspired and rightly lived if you take it bravely and gallantly, as a splendid adventure in which you are setting out into an unknown country, to meet many a joy, to find many a comrade, to win and lose many a battle."

So as you turn the pages of this book . . .

- Ask for wisdom.

- Look for wisdom.

- Contemplate wisdom.

- Embrace wisdom.

- Apply wisdom.

- Practice wisdom.

- Share wisdom.

As you seek wisdom, you'll start your journey with these twenty-one steps. And you'll soon be on your way to an exciting, purpose-filled life!

STEP ❶
PAY ATTENTION

It had been an overwhelming week.

I was going to school, doing two internships, working two jobs, volunteering at church, repairing a house built in 1902, and trying to finish a complicated doctoral dissertation. I was twenty-six years old and attempting to do much more than was realistic or even rational.

On my way home from church one beautiful spring afternoon, I looked up and noticed I was driving through a red light. Before I could even finish the thought, a car broadsided me. Glass shattered and metal crumpled. I shook my body to make sure everything was working properly. Then I went to the other car and was relieved to find out that no one was hurt.

When the police officer arrived and checked out the accident, he pulled me to the side and gave me a piece of sage advice: "When you're driving, you've got to pay attention."

I can't tell you how many times parents and teachers told me that. I heard it in anger, frustration, impatience, and sometimes even in jest. I was surprised to find that Solomon, the wisest man in the world, also used these words. "Pay attention and learn good judgment. . . . My child, pay attention to what I say. Listen carefully to my words."[1]

As a psychologist it is my job to pay attention. As soon as someone walks into my office, I focus on his or her words, tone of voice, emotions, needs, concerns, beliefs, perspective, history, relationships, openness, and body language. This requires focus, and it can be exhausting. Paying attention is not always easy; in fact, sometimes it is hard work. Yet the payoff is that we become aware of an amazing world of causes and consequences just below the surface. Life is incredible. It is rich and inspiring beyond our wildest imagination, but we have to pay attention.

I am convinced that few of us have any idea what is really happening all around us. We don't look or listen with intentionality. J. Oswald Sanders wrote, "Eyes that look are common. Eyes that see are rare." None of us sees as often as we could. We don't take time to slow down, and when we do, we still don't consider very carefully what is right in front of us. Maybe we are too distracted or lazy or worn-out. Maybe we are looking at the wrong things or in the wrong direction. José, Ortega y Gasset said, "Tell me to what you pay attention and I will tell you who you are." Sometimes we just don't know how to pay attention. Yet whatever our reasons, this is something we can change with a bit of effort. Here are four big areas where we all need to pay more attention.

REALITY

Kelly is a sixteen-year-old girl whose parents have just divorced. She feels abandoned, disappointed, scared, and trapped between two people she truly loves. Through her tears she told me, "I want to close my eyes and make it all go away." John is so afraid of the history of cancer in his family that, even though he has some serious medical symptoms, he refuses to go to a physician. Judy and James were so overwhelmed by their financial situation that they didn't open any of their mail for six months—it was just too hard to look at all the bills. During that time their electricity was turned off, their garbage service was discontinued, creditors sued them, and their house went into foreclosure. All three of these stories are true, and in each case their situation got worse because they refused to pay attention to reality.

Situations rarely get better all by themselves. Paying attention allows us to problem solve, get help, consider alternatives, or at least prepare for the worst. In his book *The Next Generation Leader*, Andy Stanley provides some rules about facing reality:

- Thou shalt not pretend.

- Thou shalt not turn a blind eye.

- Thou shalt not exaggerate.

- Thou shalt not shoot the bearer of bad news.

- Thou shalt not ignore constructive criticism.

- Thou shalt not isolate thyself.

Each of these rules is critical to facing reality. To ignore any one of them is to encourage disaster at all levels—cognitive, emotional, social, physical, and ultimately, spiritual. Situations rarely get better by themselves. If you can find the courage to face reality and take action, you will increase your chances of improving your situation and discovering a positive outcome.

An honest and correct perspective of reality protects us from avoidable disasters. It also keeps us on a path that leads to growth—a growth that fills our lives with wisdom, joy, peace, and faith, which are more valuable than all the wealth this world has to offer. M. Scott Peck writes in his best-selling book *The Road Less Traveled* that "our view of reality is like a map with which to negotiate the terrain of life. If the map is true and accurate, we will generally know where we are. . . . If the map is false and inaccurate, we generally will be lost." So open your eyes, look around, and pay attention to reality.

OPPORTUNITIES

Life is full of incredible opportunities, but most people never pay enough attention even to see them. Every day various doors of opportunity stand before us—sometimes they are frightening, inconvenient, or out of our comfort zone. Several years ago I was approached to do a daily call-in radio talk show. My schedule was full, and I had no experience with radio. I had been a successful psychologist for twenty years and had spoken to hundreds of groups, but quite frankly, the idea made me nervous. What if I was on the air and didn't know what to say? What if I made a mistake and a hundred thousand people heard it? What if I sounded foolish or uninformed? The what-if's overwhelmed me until I asked myself, *What if God just opened a door of opportunity? Are you willing to trust him and walk through it or are you going to slam it in his face?* I'm glad to say I walked through it and had an absolutely fantastic time for four and a half years, until God shut that door and opened another.

A wonderful proverb says, "When God shuts a door, he opens a window." We have all had doors closed on us, and that can be a painful experience. But a closed door simply means a new opportunity somewhere else. As

Alexander Graham Bell, the inventor of the telephone, once said, "When one door closes, another opens. But we often look so long and so regretfully upon the closed door that we do not see the one which has opened for us." We are surrounded with opportunities beyond our greatest dreams. God is patiently waiting to bless us. All we need to do is pay attention and seize the opportunities before us. Opportunities come in at least four varieties:

① **Easy opportunities:** things we feel competent at and capable of

② **Challenging opportunities:** things which stretch us and are out of our comfort zone

③ **Overwhelming opportunities:** things we can't do without the expertise or assistance of others

④ **Supernatural opportunities:** things that seem impossible (We know we can't do these things without God.)

We need to have all four of these types of opportunities in our life. Unfortunately, many of us keep gravitating to the easy opportunities, rarely slipping into the challenging or overwhelming areas. Because of this, we live stunted lives. We forget those incredible promises from the Bible: words like "With God everything is possible" and "I can do everything through Christ, who gives me strength."[2]

Knowing that God is near, we can face any and every opportunity, even if it leaves us uneasy or fearful. In this spirit, Grace Speare encourages us to "welcome every problem as an opportunity. Each moment is the great challenge, the best thing that ever happened to you. The more difficult the problem, the greater the challenge in working it out."

Every moment is a great opportunity with the possibility of being the best thing that ever happened to you. If we are willing to look to God, we will find him waiting to take us to unforgettable places of excitement and fulfillment and opportunities. So as a guard told the prophet Jeremiah when he released him from captivity, "The whole land is before you—go wherever you like."[3]

BEAUTY AND WONDER

Yesterday I went on a hike with my two sons, Dylan and Dusty, up the small creek behind our house. It was a sunny February day with a frosty nip to the air, but we were determined to go exploring. We battled through brambles, climbed over mossy rocks, and waded across chilly waters. We laughed and joked and had a great time. About a mile upstream, all three of us suddenly grew silent. We had just entered a secluded place where the creek cascaded and the mist lingered in the air. A small grove of stately cedars guarded the multiple shades of green ferns and ivy. As the sunlight filtered through the trees at the perfect angle that illuminated the water, we knew this spot was sacred. It was beautiful, incredibly beautiful.

Creation loves to surprise us in a thousand breathtaking ways that touch our hearts and invigorate our senses. The incandescent splash of oranges, yellows, and purples as the sun sets on the distant hills. The gentle melody of songbirds backed by the crashing waves of an early morning in Puerto Vallarta. The sweet and tangy strawberry freshly picked from my backyard in Oregon. The delightful fragrance of gardenia, plumeria, or jasmine on a perfectly clear star-studded Hawaiian night. The warmth of the sun on your face on a chilly morning or a brisk, cool breeze on a hot afternoon. As fourteen-year-old Anne Frank wrote in her diary, "Think of all the beauty that's still left in and around you and be happy!"

Nature is amazing. We are daily surrounded by its awe, wonder, majesty, splendor, power, and terror, but so often we fail to pay attention. Jesus tells us to "look at the lilies of the field. . . ." It's like he's telling us to stop and think about the simplest aspects of nature—the details, the fine points, the nonessentials.

A friend once asked me the purpose of all the unique, beautiful flowers that bloom in unknown meadows and are never seen by humans. My mind flashed to a hillside I stumbled upon off a narrow gravel road at the Arctic Circle in northern Iceland. It was ablaze with thousands of brilliant yellow-and-blue wildflowers. I wonder whether God creates all this beauty for his own enjoyment as well as ours. Anne Dillard wrote, "Beauty and grace are performed whether or not we will sense them. The least we can do is try to be there . . . so that creation need not play to an empty house." I want to be there, and I want to pay attention.

We have lost our sense of beauty and wonder. We have grown calloused and complacent. We have become so preoccupied with ourselves that we miss the glory of nature. Paul Simon said, "This is a world of miracles and wonders." Yet we walk amid the beauty, unaware of its magnificence and message.

Henry Ward Beecher wrote that "beauty may be said to be God's trademark in creation." Yet we often pay no attention to his handiwork and then wonder why we can't feel his presence. We need to pray with Rabbi Joshua Abraham Heschel: "Dear Lord, grant me the grace of wonder. Surprise me, amaze me, awe me in every crevice of your universe. Each day enrapture me with your marvelous things without number. I do not ask to see the reason for it all; I only ask to share the wonder of it all."

GOD MOMENTS

The book of Genesis tells the story of Jacob's dream, in which he saw a stairway that was filled with angels and reached from earth to heaven. When he awoke, he declared, "Surely the Lord is in this place, and I wasn't even aware of it!"[4] Jacob had a "God moment"—a point in time when he was keenly aware of God reaching out and touching his life. Most of us have had moments when we sensed that God had just done something amazing in our lives or when we sensed that God was present with us. Unfortunately, we frequently don't pay attention to these moments, so they come and go and are often forgotten. They should be remembered, treasured, and shared with others. They are an important part of our story and a significant reminder of God's grace.

Jim Caviezel will never forget his God moments. Jim played Jesus in the 2004 Mel Gibson movie *The Passion of the Christ*. He dangled nearly naked on a cross for weeks in bone-chilling winds during the filming. He was struck by lightning during a re-creation of the Sermon on the Mount. A fourteen-inch gash was ripped into his back when the soldiers missed their mark during scenes of Jesus' scourging. He dislocated his shoulder while carrying the cross. Through all of this he became aware of God's presence and his protection. Jim said that these experiences "forced me into the arms of God. That's the only place I can go."

In his book *The God Moment Principle*, Alan Wright discusses the following five kinds of God moments:

① **Amazing Rescues:** moments when God protected us, healed us, rescued us, or made a way out for us

② **Holy Attractions:** moments when God led us to a healthier path, enabled us to resist a temptation, or inspired us to take a higher road

③ **Unearned Blessings:** moments when God gave us an unexpected blessing or an underserved gift

④ **Revealed Truths:** moments when God spoke to us through something we heard, saw, read, or felt, and conveyed truth about himself or our life

⑤ **Valuable Adversities:** moments when God sustained us through difficult times or made us stronger through tests of adversity

If we pay attention to all the God moments in our life, we will be lifted above everyday, ordinary existence to a level of greater meaning, purpose, and perspective. Julian of Norwich, a fourteenth-century English writer, stated, "It is God's will for us to pay attention to all his past acts. . . . Only then shall we rejoice in God." God moments, whether big or small, give us a more accurate and meaningful perspective on life, while reminding us of his never-ending perspective.

THE SMALL STUFF

Mr. Crammer was my sixth-grade teacher. He was big and strong and had the meanest throwing arm I'd ever seen. One afternoon I was sitting in the back row telling jokes with my friend Dennis as Mr. Crammer was trying to teach us something about algebra. I hated algebra. Suddenly an eraser flew across the classroom and hit me smack-dab in the center of my forehead.

"Steve," came his booming voice as I rubbed my head, "I would strongly suggest that you pay attention."

"Yes, sir," I replied.

Too often we miss the important stuff of life because we don't pay attention. In the book *God Is in the Small Stuff*, Bruce and Stan insist that "if you want to improve in any area of your life, you have to pay attention to the small stuff." Sometimes the details and seemingly insignificant pieces of life can have an extremely significant impact. So besides what's been listed above, here are a few more things to pay attention to:

- the details

- people and relationships

- where you've been

- where you're going

- lessons you've learned

- consequences

- your words and tone of voice

I guess I'd also better add red lights and flying erasers. Yes, Mr. Crammer, I was listening, and I will work harder to pay attention.

STEP ❷

LIVE INTENTIONALLY

Life is full of choices.

In 1845 Henry David Thoreau chose to move out of a comfortable home to live alone in the woods in a house he built himself a mile from his nearest neighbor. He lived there for two years and two months. When asked why he would do such a thing, he replied, "I went to the woods because I wished to live deliberately . . . and not, when I came to die, discover that I had not lived. . . . I wanted to live deep and suck out all the marrow of life."

Living life intentionally makes all the difference.

Your life is the sum of all the choices you make. Madeleine L'Engle wrote, "It is the ability to choose which makes us human," and George Eliot adds, "The strongest principle of growth lies in human choice." Lack of choice leads to lack of direction, and that takes us nowhere. Not making choices or being passive gets us in a rut. The longer we stay in the rut, the more we grow stagnant. To stagnate is

- to lie dormant;

- to be inactive;

- to fail to progress;

- to exist without motion;

- to die slowly.

Choices move us forward; they cause us to grow. Our choices demonstrate who we really are. They show our character and shape our destiny.

Paul J. Meyer wrote, "Your choice is your power . . . you never know how large the impact may be from a seemingly minor choice." One simple choice can send out ripples that change your life and the lives of those around you.

I haven't seen Danny since we were both teenagers. He had been my next-door neighbor and grade-school buddy. He was smart, athletic, handsome, and a natural-born leader. When I ran into him again after many years apart, I gave him a big hug and said, "It's so good to see you. What have you been up to all these years?"

"You don't want to know," Danny told me as he looked at the ground. "I've spent a lot of time wandering from town to town, looking for work. I've picked apples, mowed lawns, pumped gas. But most of the time I've spent in jail."

"What happened?" I asked, shocked.

He looked me in the eyes with a tear running down his cheek.

"It's simple, really," he said. "When I was a kid, I had two close friends. You were my positive influence. Doug was my negative influence. When I was fourteen, I chose to spend my time hanging out with Doug. That was the dumbest choice I've ever made, and I have paid for it for the past thirty years."

I gave Danny another hug and said, "But today you can start making different choices." He smiled and said, "Thanks."

Choices are incredibly powerful, but they can also be frightening because intentional, proactive choices involve a risk. Yet it is only through risking that you can grow. Helen Keller put it very simply: "Life is either a daring adventure or nothing."

Life is a journey, and each step is a choice. Some people refuse to start, or they panic along the way and stop. Others step forward randomly with their eyes shut. Yet what I encourage you to do is to step intentionally with your eyes wide open. Solomon wrote, "Look straight ahead, and fix your eyes on what lies before you."[1] As Michael Molinos, a seventeenth-century Spanish martyr, wrote: "When a man sets out on a journey to a great city, every step he takes is voluntary; he does not need to say, 'I wish to go to the great city, I wish to go to the great city.' That first step is an indication of his intention. He journeys without saying it, but he cannot journey without intending it." Determine your destination, your direction, and the best way to get there. Then choose to start your journey. This is the beginning of a thousand exciting choices.

The setting for the movie *The Matrix* is a time in the future where most humans have shut their minds to what's really happening in the world. When the character Neo realizes this, he faces a choice that will change his life dramatically. He can take a blue pill, forget everything that's happened, and return to his comfortable, but false, life. Or he can take a red pill, wake up, and face a tough reality—but also have a chance to save all of humanity. Maybe our choices aren't as big as Neo's, but they are significant. We all must choose what to do with our time, energy, ability, influence, and resources. These choices aren't always easy or obvious, but they are fundamental to everything else. So what color of pill will you take?

CHOOSING TO FOLLOW GOD

Live intentionally rather than passively or haphazardly. As the apostle Paul says in Ephesians, "Don't act thoughtlessly, but understand what the Lord wants you to do."[2] Consider your options. Don't let the pressures or expectations of those around you force your hand. Colin Powell warned, "Be careful what you choose. You may get it." Think through the cost and consequences of your choices, but also recognize the cost and consequences of not choosing. There are times we all need help with our choices regardless of our age or maturity. So find a friend, a counselor, or a pastor who can give you perspective and wisdom.

I knew a woman named Sally who was just coasting through life. She always did just enough to get by, living on automatic pilot, safe within her comfort zone. She didn't challenge herself, and therefore she didn't accomplish much. But that's okay with her because she didn't expect much. Sally was a nice person, but I feel such a sadness for her. She had no spark or joy for life.

My friend Allison is just the opposite. She loves to try new things, takes risks, and constantly stretches herself. Allison is determined to fill each day with excitement and exuberance. She chooses to live intentionally, and as a result, she loves life.

Lillian Carter, the mother of former president Jimmy Carter, was a lot like Allison. At sixty-eight, she went to rural India to work as a nurse with the Peace Corps. At seventy-eight, she crossed the country as an energetic and active member of her son's campaign team. At eighty-five, she stated, "Sure, I'm for helping the elderly. I'm going to be old myself someday." Lillian insisted on choosing life, and that is exactly how she lived, right up to the day of her death.

God wants us to live a full and abundant life. Jesus said, "My purpose is to give life in all its fullness."[3] He wants us to make positive and proactive choices so we can fulfill our life purpose. Thomas Merton wrote, "We must make choices that enable us to fulfill the deepest capacities of our real selves." God knows our capacities, and he wants us to let him use them. When he asks us to follow him, he wants us to stop what we're doing and step out. It might be uncomfortable and challenging and frightening, but God's way is ultimately the best and most satisfying way. He asked

- Noah to build an ark;
- Abraham to leave his home;
- Moses to free his people;
- David to face Goliath.

None of these were easy choices, but each of them led to something surprising. Noah was saved from a flood. Abraham became the ancestor of the Jews. Moses led the Israelites across the Red Sea to the Promised Land. David defeated a giant and proved God's power. Without taking risks, none of these individuals would have accomplished what they did. Each of these choices by these ordinary people set in motion a series of events that made their lives extraordinary.

FREEDOM FROM FEAR

What keeps most people from living intentionally and making life-changing decisions is fear. Moses encouraged his people to "be strong and courageous! Do not be afraid. . . . For the Lord your God will personally go ahead of you. He will neither fail you nor abandon you."[4] Take a stand and choose courage. Courage is not the absence of fear; it is taking positive action in spite of your fears. Archbishop Desmond Tutu said, "Being courageous . . . means acting as you know you must, even though you are undeniably afraid." If we're courageous, we'll seriously consider risk but not allow the risk to paralyze us. We might need to shift our path, but we won't need to run away or hide.

Courage moves us forward. It allows us to face life head-on and live life to the fullest. Ralph Waldo Emerson wrote, "Whatever you do, you need courage. Whatever course you decide upon, there is always someone to tell you that you are wrong. There are always difficulties arising that tempt you to believe your critics are right. To map out a course of action and to follow it to an end requires some of the same courage that a soldier needs."

Not to choose courage is to cave in to cowardice or mediocrity. Charles Crismier, in his book *Renewing the Soul of America*, writes about nine types of courage:

① **Courage of conscience:** to do what is right
② **Courage to confirm:** to do what the law requires of you
③ **Courage to communicate:** to speak on issues of importance
④ **Courage to consider:** to rethink preconceived notions
⑤ **Courage to care:** to take personal responsibility and show love for others
⑥ **Courage to confront:** to stand up to untruth and injustice
⑦ **Courage to challenge:** to change the way you've always done it if it has been wrong
⑧ **Courage to correct:** to change your own behavior if it is wrong
⑨ **Courage to confess:** to acknowledge your personal wrongs toward others and God

On January 13, 1982, a fierce blizzard struck Washington DC. At 3:59 that afternoon, Air Florida Flight 90 clipped the 14th Street bridge after takeoff and crashed into the icy waters of the Potomac River.

Lenny Skutnik, a twenty-eight-year-old office worker, had just gotten off work. He was an ordinary guy, going home to his wife and two children. But at that moment, he saw the explosion and heard a young woman screaming for help. Without hesitation, he jumped out of his car and dove into the freezing water.

Lenny's act of courage saved the life of twenty-two-year-old Priscilla Tirado. This story got a lot of national attention, but every day there are hundreds of similar acts of courage that slip by, unnoticed. Unnoticed, but not insignificant.

Robert pulled a two-year-old from the path of an oncoming car. Todd and Matt knocked on the doors of a burning apartment building. Sam befriended a special-needs student in his classroom. Clair convinced a friend that suicide is not the answer. Lori forgave her father for physically and sexually abusing her. Jody faced life with her three young children after the death of her husband. Dylan stood up to three young bullies who were attacking his best friend.

These are just a few of the acts of courage that happen all around us every day. Our choices make all the difference. They can make us or destroy us; they can connect us with others or alienate us; they can build our character or tarnish it. They can lift us above our circumstances or sink us into the deepest despair. Some choices seem natural; others are made by sheer, gut-wretching willpower. But we do have choices. Living intentionally is broader than making choices to act a certain way or take a certain course. It involves making choices about our attitude.

ACCENTUATE THE POSITIVE

I've met all sorts of people in very difficult situations with physical handicaps, painful marriages, broken hearts, financial ruin, and seemingly hopeless futures. And yet they hold a positive, uplifting attitude. I don't know how they do it. William James wrote, "The greatest discovery of my generation is that human beings can alter their lives by altering their attitude of mind." Abraham Lincoln said it more simply: "Most folks are about as happy as they make up their minds to be."

I asked one woman who had been abandoned by her husband how she kept such a positive attitude. She had three small children, no job, no home, no friends, no good options. She lived in her car and ate at a local homeless shelter. She smiled and said, "I'm not dead, my children love me, and things can't get any worse." You can always choose your attitude. John Maxwell wrote, "We choose what attitudes we have right now. And it's a continuing choice." In fact, your attitude is the most important decision you make each and every day. Your attitude might very well set the stage for every other choice you make.

As for me, I want to make strong, affirming choices. I want to live life to the fullest with courage and a great attitude. I don't want to waste my time or miss the mark or wake up someday only to wonder what I have been doing the past ten years. I want to stretch and grow and love and in some way, no matter how small, leave this world a better place than when I entered it. I want to reach out and dig deep and shine bright. I want to know God and celebrate all there is to celebrate.

So join me on this journey. Wake up. Choose to live with purpose and direction. Choose to live intentionally and make choices daily to affirm who you are and what you believe. Here are a few of the choices that must be made:

- Choosing to start

- Choosing to prepare

- Choosing to risk

- Choosing your path

- Choosing your actions

- Choosing your dreams

- Choosing your attitude

- Choosing your priorities

- Choosing your battles

- Choosing your courage

- Choosing to live life to its fullest

- Choosing God

Remember, not to choose is to choose. Ed Rowell says it this way in *Go the Distance:* "We will never get another chance at today. If we don't make intentional choices, based on our understanding of God's place for our lives, we will be consumed by the purposes of other people. It's time to focus. We can't afford to wait until tomorrow. Set your course today and stick to it."

Yesterday I spoke to Jody, a twenty-three-year-old college student. She has a vibrancy and excitement about her that is contagious. Her dreams are clear and her plans to achieve them are strategic.

"How do you start?" I asked.

With a soft smile and steely stare she said, "You just have to go for it."

STEP ❸

KNOW YOURSELF

You are utterly amazing!

You are a miracle and a mystery!

You are "fearfully and wonderfully made."[1]

Now if all of this is true, why don't more people look inside and get to know who they are? As a psychologist, I have concluded that most people live their lives without ever knowing themselves at anything but a fairly superficial level. Yet how can you truly connect with anyone else or even God unless you have at least some inkling of who you are? How can you make informed choices, grow as a person, or compassionately reach out to others unless you know what is inside your heart? Socrates was right when he said over two thousand years ago, "The unexamined life is not worth living." Marcus Aurelius, a Roman emperor, said that a wise man gives himself "frequent self-examinations."

Maturity requires self-awareness, but this is not to be confused with self-absorption. To be self-aware is to acknowledge who we are before God. It is to look beyond outward appearance to the heart, thanking God for each of our assets and liabilities. As we do so, we can yield our abilities and talents to him, while he builds upon our wounds and weaknesses. Self-awareness allows us to see ourselves as God sees us. On the other hand, to be self-absorbed is to look upon ourselves as either more or less significant than reality dictates. Self-absorption stunts our growth, marginalizes those around us, and makes God our servant.

Knowing yourself does not come naturally or easily. We spend so much of our time distracted and overwhelmed by what happens *around* us that we don't take the time to consider what is *in* us. Who we really are deep under our skin is a bundle of beauty, terror, consistency, ambiguity, arrogance, and insecurity. We each embody the sublime contradiction of being created in the image of God but formed from the dust of the earth. As the image of God we are creative, intelligent, and spiritual with the capacity for choice and moral excellence. Yet as the dust of the earth we have limitations and weaknesses with the potential for woundedness, failure, and evil.

POTENTIAL FOR GOOD AND EVIL

As a college student I went to a seminar taught by the late Elisabeth Kubler-Ross. She said, "We all have deep within our hearts a little Adolf Hitler, who, given the right circumstances, is capable of the worst forms of hatred and destruction. We also possess a little Mother Teresa, capable of the most wonderful acts of charity and selflessness." Her words shocked and fascinated me.

We may not like to admit it, but we are this strange combination of both good and evil, light and dark, hope and doom, health and sickness. Our attempt to understand ourselves begins with accepting, and even embracing, these opposites. It is only then that we can give ourselves fully to God and let him transform us into what glorifies him most. Yet, to even look at some of these inner contradictions makes many of us uncomfortable. We want everything tucked into neat little boxes that explain all our feelings, words, and actions. Our personalities contain many patterns and tendencies, but there are also disturbing loose strings that don't fit into our little boxes like they should. The first step in knowing yourself is accepting that each of us has weaknesses as well as strengths.

YOUR WEAKNESSES

Everyone dislikes parts of themselves. To be human is to be imperfect. Jean Vanier wrote, "Growth begins when we begin to accept our own weakness." We all have weaknesses and limitations at every level (physical, emotional, cognitive, social, and spiritual). To deny these is to live a lie. Pablo Casals wrote, "The main thing in life is not to be afraid to be human." Even the apostle Paul says, "I take pleasure in my weaknesses."[2] Yet Paul goes on to say that "when I am weak, I am strong" because that is when we must look to God and rely on his strength to get us through the challenges of life. Therefore, there might even be times when God gives us a "thorn in the flesh" like he gave to Paul, so that we might not grow too independent or self-sufficient.

Weaknesses show themselves in many ways. Some appear through our failures, frustrations, and fears. Others display themselves in our confusion and uncertainty. Still others haunt us through our woundedness. You cannot live without being wounded, whether sexually, physically, verbally, emotionally, socially, spiritually, or by your choices.

However these wounds might have been inflicted, they are painful and leave scars that last a lifetime. We are all wounded. Some hide it better than others. Some lie about it, either to themselves or to those surrounding them. Yet the truth remains that we are all weak and broken and wounded.

Every day we fall. It may be a slight stumble or a full face-on-the-floor flop. Our lives are replete with these all-too-real reminders of our humanity that leave each of us hoping for grace and dreaming of mercy.

Knowing yourself involves owning your weaknesses, then being vulnerable enough to reveal them to others. In many ways the greatest gift we can give is our weakness, our brokenness, and our woundedness. This gift allows us to reach out with an understanding and compassion that we might not have otherwise. Someone who has a history of sexual abuse might have a better understanding of young girls who have experienced the same sort of nightmare. A person who struggled with reading as a child often makes a great teacher because he or she knows just how hard some students must work to get through each class.

Without our limitations, we might very well lack the motivation, insight, and determination to help others overcome their own limitations. It's our weakness that makes us real and connects us with others. Yet most of all it forces us to lean upon God, not only for his strength, but also as the source of all grace and mercy. Harriet Beecher Stowe, author of *Uncle Tom's Cabin*, wrote, "Many a humble soul will be amazed to find that the seed it sowed in weakness, in the dust of daily life, has blossomed into immortal flowers under the eye of the Lord." God can redeem our failures. And we learn the truth of what Dallas Willard writes in *The Divine Conspiracy*: "Nothing irredeemable has happened to us or can happen to us on our way to our destiny in God's full world."

YOUR STRENGTHS

God has wrapped up something of value inside each one of us, yet most of us are more aware of our weaknesses than our strengths. Few will argue that we all have weaknesses, but our strengths seem harder to admit. An important part of knowing ourselves is facing the fact that "God has given us different gifts for doing certain things well."[3]

Many struggle with whether they actually have special abilities or gifts because they have not yet discovered them. As I've worked with people, I've noticed that abilities tend to fall into ten general categories. Everyone is gifted in at least one of the following:

1. **Verbal:** You have a way with words. You are good at using language to express yourself, whether through speaking or writing.

2. **Mathematical:** You are good at using and figuring numbers.

3. **Logical:** You have the ability to sequentially, step-by-step work through a problem, project, or issue to get to an end point.

4. **Social:** You are good at connecting with people and helping them feel comfortable.

5. **Physical:** You have athletic abilities that allow you to do well in sports or areas that require strength, balance, or coordination.

6. **Mechanical:** You enjoy putting things together, taking them apart, and fixing them.

7. **Musical:** You are good at writing, conducting, engineering, or performing music.

8. **Visual:** You have an eye for things like color, design, texture, shape, and size. You can see how things fit together.

9. **Personal:** You have an understanding and sensitivity toward the emotions, motives, cognitions, and other psychological constructs that make people do what they do.

10. **Organizational:** You are able to create or restructure order so that it is more effective and accomplishes whatever goals you set.

You have at least one of these strengths. It may be in a raw form, and it may require training or developing or polishing, but it does exist. For some people, their strength is obvious. For others, it may be temporarily hidden. If you're not sure where your abilities lie, these simple questions might help you identify your strength:

- What areas are you naturally good at?

- What areas are fun and exciting to you?

- What areas do you get the most compliments in?

These are the areas in which you have been gifted. If you are still stuck, ask a friend or someone who knows you well to give you his or her opinion.

Once you've discovered and accepted your strengths, it is important to make sure you are using what God has granted you. Pope John XXIII said, "Concern yourself not with your failures, but with all that is still possible for you to do." Take your ability and find a place to use it. If you are mathematical, get involved with numbers. If you are social, surround yourself with people. If you are organizational, start organizing. The saddest thing I see is when people spend most of their time doing things they struggle with rather than what they're good at.

To live a great life, spend as much time as you can doing what you're best at. In so doing, you will feel excited, energized, and fulfilled. Likewise, too much time spent in your areas of weakness will exhaust, frustrate, and suck the life out of you. Marilyn vos Savant, a woman with the one of the highest recorded IQs in the world, wrote, "Success is achieved by developing our strengths, not by eliminating our weaknesses."

ONE OF A KIND

Like snowflakes and fingerprints, each of us is one of a kind. Besides our weaknesses and strengths, we possess a host of neutral characteristics. We are an amazing combination of needs, beliefs, tendencies, emotions, sensitivities, perceptions, and passions. Mixed together with just the right amount of each, you are a miracle God has specially created.

In order to understand the gift of who you are, you must look inside the package. Aime Cesaire, a twentieth-century poet from Martinique, said that "the secret to staying young is to never stop searching for yourself." Yet to know yourself is not always easy. It is often your most difficult journey. Just when you think you know who you are, you surprise yourself by something you do or say. These surprises are sometimes splendid and sometimes shocking, yet they are a part of the marvelous mystery of who you are. Embrace yourself. God made you. Sure you need repairs and improvements, but that's true of all of us. Accept yourself, yet always be open to growth, allowing God to stretch you into all that you can be.

On a shelf in my office sits a brass kaleidoscope with double wheels of different types of stained glass. Some of the glass pieces in these wheels are like beautiful, sparkling jewels, while others are quite ordinary. As I look through the eyepiece, I am amazed to see how these elements come together to create such an awe-inspiring collection of patterns. I love to sit back, spin these wheels, and get lost in the ever-changing images. One day my kaleidoscope slipped out of a little boy's fingers. My heart sank when I saw a large crack across one of the glass wheels, yet to my surprise this crack made the designs more intriguing and intricate than before.

My cracked kaleidoscope reminds me of the human condition. We are all made of beautiful strengths and ordinary traits, but it's the cracks of weakness that give us character. Instead of decreasing our value, the cracks make us all the more interesting. These cracks also force us to turn to God or to turn back to God, for he is the only one who can meld them into wonder-filled patterns and keep them from shattering into useless shards of glass. So study your kaleidoscope, and look deep into its patterns. You might be surprised at all you can see.

STEP ❹
KEEP BALANCED

"I can't do it!"

"Oh yes you can," Aunt Sandy insisted.

My six-year-old hands gripped the handlebars of my bicycle, and my body tensed. "Please don't let go," I begged.

"You've got to learn to ride a bicycle sometime."

"But the road is too bumpy, and I'll crash."

"Hold on!" Aunt Sandy called as she ran alongside my bike. Then she gave it a strong push.

I went sailing down the road, holding on for dear life. I tried to reach the pedals so I could put on the brakes, but my legs were too short. The bike picked up a little speed as it went down a slight slope, and I panicked. I closed my eyes and prayed that I wouldn't die.

Crash!!!

I went directly into a tree. The bike fell over, and I scraped up my knee pretty badly. Through my tears I cried, "I did it. I kept my balance."

Aunt Sandy shook her head. "But you have to keep your eyes open."

When you first learn to ride a bike, keeping your balance is hard, but as you develop confidence and experience it gets easier. Now when I climb on a bike, I don't even think about keeping my balance. It just comes naturally.

Walking, jogging, skateboarding, climbing, reaching, and almost every simple movement you make requires balance. Every morning as you roll out of bed to stand up, sensors and receptors in your muscles send lightning-fast messages to your brain, which returns with the appropriate responses to small stabilizer muscles in your feet. This process is called balance. Without it you will stumble, trip, flail, and definitely fall.

To a healthy, growing person, balance is much more important than physical coordination. It has to do with respecting each aspect of who you are. It means that you recognize the five key parts of yourself:

① mind
② heart
③ relationships
④ body
⑤ spirit

Each of these parts is equally wonderful and individually holy. Each needs its time and focus. We are indeed the sum of our parts. After all, the word health comes from an old English word meaning "whole." As Pope John Paul II said, "Man always travels along precipices. . . . His truest obligation is to keep balance."

Ever since I was a small child I have been fascinated by starfish. I can remember searching the rocks and tide pools of Cannon Beach near my home in Oregon for these amazing creatures. One day I found a starfish that was missing an arm. It looked strange and lopsided; it had lost its symmetry and balance. It was still alive and held much of its beauty, but it just didn't look right. We are each like a five-armed starfish. We can still function without an arm or two, but it will be obvious something important is missing.

Each of your five "arms" impacts every other arm. Your mind informs your heart, calming or enflaming your emotions. Your heart touches your relationships, pulling them toward you, pushing them away, or positioning you against them. Your relationships influence your body, relaxing or stressing it, draining or energizing it. Your body affects your spirit, lifting it up or weighing it down. The repercussions of this process can happen in reverse or in any other order, but the interdependence shows how important it is that you respect and care for each of these five arms.

TAKE CARE OF YOUR MIND

Your mind matters. Through your mind you form beliefs that help you navigate through life. You might come to believe that you can't trust strangers or that hard work is the core of success or that broccoli might kill you. As you face the joys and hurts of existence, your beliefs are tested. These convictions become a road map and dictionary for how to approach whatever you may face. As a road map they give you direction; as a dictionary they help you define and interpret your experiences. Over time you develop beliefs about every aspect of life, and these beliefs are reinforced through your attitudes, words, and actions.

If your mind becomes imbalanced or your thinking faulty, you are headed for trouble. Our decisions and choices are often based on our beliefs. With irrational, immature, or untrue beliefs, we steer our lives onto the rocks. Thoughts like, *God is dead, Nothing really matters, People are all idiots,* or *I'm going to do whatever I feel like whenever I feel like doing it* can lead to danger and depression. To evaluate your thinking, questioning and challenging each belief will help you to correct your life course and re-direct it into deep harbors, where the storms of reality don't do perma-nent damage.

Rational, mature, and true beliefs keep us on track in every aspect of our life. They also lead to wisdom. For this reason, I daily attempt to nur-ture and reinforce right thinking. I hold strong to beliefs like "God is good," "Prayer is powerful," "Loving others builds positive relation-ships," and "Hard work pays off." These beliefs may be simple, but they keep me strong and lead me to the best ports of call. As I take care of my mind, I also try to remember that even good thinking isolated from the other four aspects of personality can have unfavorable consequences. Healthy people must consider the impact their heart, body, spirit, and re-lationships have on all they do. As we embrace right thinking, we develop wisdom. After all, the challenge for all of us is to use wisely what God has so graciously given us.

As we balance our mind with our heart and the other aspects of our identity, we must also find the balance point within the mind. Anti-intel-lectualism is just as dangerous as over-intellectualism. The Bible provides six methods to keep your mind healthy:

① **Renew your mind** by correcting faulty thinking.[1]
② **Stretch your mind** through meditating on God's creation, unfailing love, actions, wonders, principles, commandments, and promises.[2]

③ **Focus your mind** by thinking about what is good and positive and right.[3]

④ **Fill your mind** with wisdom, understanding, good planning, and insight.[4]

⑤ **Train your mind** to recognize the difference between right and wrong.[5]

⑥ **Examine your mind** by checking your motives and affections.[6]

TAKE CARE OF YOUR HEART

In the book of Proverbs, Solomon talks a lot about the heart. He says, "As a face is reflected in water, so the heart reflects the real person."[7] He also advises to "guard your heart above all else, for it determines the course of your life."[8] Your heart can become hard or broken, anxious or angry or jealous. Your heart can also be cheerful or peaceful, compassionate or thankful or pure. Every day you experience a variety of emotions, which shows that you are alive and responding to life. People without emotions lose their spark. They become like the tin man in The Wizard of Oz, empty and hollow and not quite human. As Helen Keller once said, "The best and most beautiful things in life . . . must be felt with the heart."

Your heart is precious, but at times it can hurt and trap and confuse you. Here are a few ground rules for dealing with your emotions:

Listen to your emotions. Don't be afraid of them; they are telling you something important about yourself. To deny or ignore your feelings is to isolate yourself from your own heart, those who wish to relate to you, and God himself.

Accept your emotions. Don't reject your feelings or tell yourself that you shouldn't feel what you are feeling. Emotions can be messy and at times embarrassing or frustrating, but they are genuine.

Manage your emotions. Be honest with these feelings; don't minimize or exaggerate them. Don't let them manage or control you. Let your mind and heart work together for a balance between the two. When your heart gets stuck in fear or bitterness or depression, you may need to look beyond your feelings to your spiritual core. This is where faith and prayer can lift you above the emotional struggles that can easily pull you down.

As the apostle Paul writes in Ephesians, "I pray that your hearts will be flooded with light."[9]

TAKE CARE OF YOUR RELATIONSHIPS

We need people. Frequently they hurt us, make us angry, let us down, break our heart, and drive us crazy, but we still need people. Loneliness is one of the most painful and disabling emotions we can feel. In the Garden of Eden God said, "It is not good for the man to be alone.[10] Relationships keep us from being trapped inside of ourselves. They help us to stretch and grow and mature. They also protect us when difficulties come. Solomon reminds us that "if one person falls, the other can reach out and help. But someone who falls alone is in real trouble."[11]

Relationships can nurture us at various levels. Healthy relationships at their best should consistently provide the following six elements:

① **Connection:** Spending time with others protects us from loneliness and self-absorption. Connecting reaches out to others and allows others to reach out to us. This can be done by walking together, working together, or even going out to lunch together. Your options are only limited by your imagination.

② **Care and concern:** Showing a sensitivity to those around us is at the core of being a loving person. Caring about others and being concerned when they face difficulties keeps us from becoming hard-hearted. Sometimes simply showing a genuine interest in someone can help to build a valuable relationship.

③ **Comfort:** One of the best ways to build relationships is to come alongside someone who is facing a hard time and offer him or her words of encouragement or simply a shoulder to cry on. We all need comfort at some time in our life, and we all know someone who would appreciate it if we sacrificed our time or resources in order to make a positive impact on that person's life.

④ **Communication:** Sharing our thoughts and feelings with others brings closeness in a way that few things can. Truly listening will then deepen that closeness. Every relationship requires regular, positive communication in order to grow. Whether it is face-to-face, in an e-mail, or through the telephone, don't neglect communication.

⑤ **Celebration:** Appreciate life and celebrate with those in your life. We are all drawn to celebrations, laughter, and joy. So don't be afraid to share your excitement and enthusiasm. Celebrate life, celebrate faith, celebrate each other, and celebrate all that God has done for you.

⑥ **Creation of community:** As we consistently work to implement each of these things in the lives of those around us, we will begin to create community. Our lives will become woven together as we share the good times, sad time, difficult times, embarrassing times, joyful times, and growing times. A healthy community is truly committed to one another—no matter what.

Although these are significant elements, the most important aspect of relationships is love. In his modern classic *The Purpose-Driven Life*, Rick Warren asserts that "life is all about love." He goes on to say that "life without love is really worthless." Jesus commands us to "love your neighbor as yourself."[12] It's impossible to love apart from relationships.

TAKE CARE OF YOUR BODY

The body each of us was born with has certain characteristics and tendencies. We inherit specific genetic data which, in part, shape who we are by designating things like physical appearance, natural abilities, and personality traits. Some of these we like, some we don't really appreciate. We also have the ability to develop certain aspects of what we have inherited. We might strengthen our muscles, learn to play a musical instrument, or redeem certain negative aspects of our personality. Unfortunately we must also deal with traumas, diseases, accidents, deprivations, and poor choices that impact our physical well-being. Some people have it easier than others and that might not be fair, but as my mother said many times, "Life is not fair."

We might not be able to control everything about our body or the factors that impact it. Yet there is much we can do. Taking care of ourselves is a statement of respect and thankfulness for what God has given us.

Moses tells us to "number our days."[13] We should use our time wisely and take care of our bodies so they are as strong and healthy as they can be. A healthy body allows for a healthy mind and heart. It gives us a freedom to reach out to others and to God because we feel better, have more energy, and are less self-focused. An unhealthy body forces us inward to care for our own diseases and disabilities. Most physicians agree that the basics of taking care of your body involve the following:

- exercise and fitness

- good rest

- drinking plenty of water

- eating fruits and vegetables

- avoiding (or limiting) alcohol, refined sugars, fatty junk foods, and tobacco

- controlling your weight

- seeing a physician for regular checkups

In most situations, taking care of your body will give you a longer life and a better quality of life. It will allow you to participate in a greater number of activities with a better attitude and fewer limitations. You will have a clearer mind, a more positive heart, a more loving countenance, and a less distracted spirit.

TAKE CARE OF YOUR SPIRIT

Albert Schweitzer was concerned that many, if not most, people suffer from what he called the "sleeping sickness of the soul." In our physical, materialistic, rational, and self-absorbed culture, have we lost our soul and spirit? Have we grown blind and numb to the spiritual universe that surrounds us? Are we like the servant at Dothan?

In one of my favorite stories of Scripture, a servant wakes up one morning to see enemy troops, horses, and chariots everywhere. He panics and cries out to his master, the prophet Elisha, "What will we do now?" Elisha reassures him not to worry, but the servant is still quite frightened. Elisha then prays for God to "open his eyes and let him see!" The servant is amazed to observe a mighty angelic force of horses and chariots of fire between himself and the enemy.[14] We all need God to help us to see.

One of the most effective ways to open our spiritual eyes is through prayer. Without prayer our spirit shrivels and dies. Mother Teresa said, "Prayer is putting ourselves in the hands of God." Bruce Wilkinson wrote, "Prayer is a path to God's blessing." Martin Luther said that "prayer is the mightiest of all weapons that created natures can wield." Prayer is our connection to and communication with God. It is not powerful because of anything we do but because of who God is. It has such great significance in this universe because God listens, is touched, and chooses to respond to our stumbling words.

Prayer is our lifeline to God and to reality. In many ways, it is the secret to opening our spiritual eyes, meeting our spiritual needs, and energizing our spiritual passions. Prayer is a necessity to our spirit, just as air is a necessity to our body. Because of this, the more we pray, the stronger, the healthier, and the more balanced we can be.

The brilliant writer G. K. Chesterton wrote, "You say grace before meals. All right. But I say grace before the concert and the opera, and grace before the play and pantomine, and grace before I open a book, and grace before sketching, painting, swimming, fencing, boxing, walking, playing, dancing, and grace before I dip the pen in the ink."

Another way to open our spiritual eyes and nurture our spirit is what Brother Lawrence called "practicing the presence of God." Brother Lawrence washed pots and pans in a monastery in Paris, France, during the seventeenth century. His desire was to foster an awareness of God's closeness in the midst of every simple act he did—whether it was making an omelette, sweeping the floor, or serving breakfast to his colleagues. Brother Lawrence found God everywhere and acknowledged that presence without interruption. His close friend Joseph de Beaufort wrote, "Brother Lawrence insisted that, to be constantly aware of God's presence, it is necessary to form the habit of continually talking with Him throughout the day. To think that we must abandon conversation with Him in order to deal with the world is erroneous. Instead, as we nourish our souls by seeing God in His exaltation, we will derive a great joy at being His." Therefore, set reminders throughout your everyday life—when you wash a dish or stop at a red light or get a phone call—that become triggers to think about God and be more fully aware of his presence.

Brother Lawrence definitely knew how to take care of his spirit. We all need to cry out with David, "Renew a right spirit within me."[15] Prayer and practicing the presence of God will certainly set you on the right path to spiritual balance.

Balance is hard to define, but you know when you have it. More accurately, you know when you've lost it. When you've lost your balance

- your mind can't think right;

- your heart feels out of control;

- your relationships grow painful;

- your body will trip or fall;

- your spirit seems distant from God.

Balance is the key to growth. When you life is balanced, you'll have better perspective, peace, and a sense of purpose. It's these things that will help you stay above the drama that often plays out in life's everyday activities.

STEP ❺
LET GO

It had been a long and dangerous journey.

Frodo's mission was to carry the Ring of Power to Mount Doom in Mordor, where it could be destroyed. Now he stands, along with his trusted companion, Sam, at the edge of the fiery abyss. But he hesitates, battling with himself about throwing the ring into the flames.

"What are you waiting for?" Sam cries out to Frodo in the 2003 movie *Return of the King*. "What are you waiting for? Just let go."

Still Frodo struggles. He knows Sam is right, but with the alluring ring in his hand it doesn't seem that simple. It takes a deadly attack from Gollum to wrench the ring from Frodo's grasp. Finally the ring is destroyed, and everybody watching the movie sighs. In the book of the same title, J. R. R. Tolkien describes how letting go of the ring impacted Frodo: "In his eyes there was peace now . . . his burden was taken away . . . he was himself again, he was free."

Holding on to certain things can hurt you. They can

- distort your mind;

- harden your heart;

- push away your relationships;

- damage your body;

- block your spirit.

As Frodo discovered, things that seem small can bring a big burden. Frequently we don't fully understand how large the burden is until we let it go.

I don't like taking out the trash. But whenever the garbage can under the sink gets full, I take it to the big can in the garage. Then every Tuesday night I wheel the big can out to the curb. If I decided not to take out the trash for a month or two, garbage would pile up and a distinct odor would permeate my house. Letting go is like taking out the garbage. There are at least four things that we all need to regularly let go of: the past, anger, worry, and material possessions.

THE PAST

We all have hurts in our past. For some the hurts are ordinary, for others they are overwhelming. Every day I work with good people who have had horrible things happen to them. These hurts can create deep wounds that shape how one views life and responds to it. The death of a parent, a divorce, sexual or physical abuse, rejection, neglect, humiliation, failure, or any other number of crises can crush one's personality. These are tragic events, but allowing them to trap us in the past is even more tragic. Millions of people in this world are so stuck in the past that they have not been able to grow emotionally beyond the age when they experienced their trauma.

Letting go of our hurts is not always easy. Isaiah says to "forget the former things; do not dwell on the past."[1] At first this might seem like shallow, insensitive advice, but look closer. To forget the past, you must not dwell on it. The key to letting go of your hurts is to

- admit them;

- confront them;

- accept them;

- understand them;

- share them;

- use them;

- thank God for them;

- look beyond them.

The key to not being trapped in your past is doing what the apostle Paul says: "I am still not all I should be but I am bringing all my energies to bear on this one thing: Forgetting the past and looking forward to what lies ahead, I strain to reach the end of the race and receive the prize for which God is calling us up to heaven."[2] The past is unchangeable, but the future is a place of hope.

The past holds its share of regrets. If we could live our life over knowing what we now know, we would all do certain things differently. We all have regrets. They are inevitable and unchangeable, but they are also forgivable and instructive. Seek forgiveness from those you have hurt, and in the process forgive yourself. Then learn from the past. Change those destructive habits, and warn others not to repeat your mistakes. Stop beating yourself up. We have all done stupid and hurtful things that we hope no one ever discovers. If we have confessed these to God, he has erased our foolishness. He no longer holds it against us, so we shouldn't either. Let go of your regrets, and focus on your future. M. Scott Peck said that contentment is "being at peace with unchangeable circumstances, choices, and mistakes of your past." Letting go gives you peace.

ANGER

Anger is dangerous. It can destroy you and those around you. It can destroy marriages, families, friendships, and jobs. Solomon said, "Fools vent their anger."[3] Throughout the book of Proverbs he also said that unmanaged anger acts restlessly, leads to foolishness, creates quarrels, alienates those you love, and steals your peace. David, Solomon's father, simply wrote, "Stop being angry!"[4] But anger doesn't always stop easily.

Anger happens when we have unmet expectations, when we believe we deserve certain things, but those things don't happen the way we think they should. We get angry when we believe we must succeed at all we do, that others must meet our criteria of behavior, or that we deserve to be treated a certain way. Unrealistic expectations get us nowhere except more upset. So counter your expectations with four simple rules that apply both to how you deal with others and how you deal with yourself:

① Be patient.
② Be realistic.
③ Be understanding.
④ Be humble.

Whether you call it getting mad, frustrated, bothered, irritated, ticked off, provoked, resentful, displeased, or annoyed, it's all the same. Anger isn't worth holding on to. Here are ten parts to letting go:

① **Admit your emotions:** If you're angry, be honest with yourself about it. Don't deny it, ignore it, or bury it.

② **Evaluate your anger:** Ask yourself, *What triggers my anger? When am I most likely to feel anger? How do I express my anger?*

③ **Choose your perception:** Slow down and put your frustration in perspective. Frame the situation in as positive a way as you can.

④ **Calm down:** If your anger is getting out of control, lower your voice, sit down, and breathe deeply. If you still can't calm down, remove yourself from the situation.

⑤ **Watch your words and actions:** When you're angry, it is easy to say things you will later regret. Once those words and actions are out, you can never take them back.

⑥ **Work out your anger:** Physical activity can reduce your anger. Go for a drive, weed a garden, paint a room, write a letter, or take a long walk.

⑦ **Talk about your anger:** Take responsibility for your feelings. Be direct and honest without blaming or attacking. The better you can communicate about your anger, the more you can control it.

⑧ **Don't let the sun go down on your anger:** Resolve your anger as soon as possible. Unresolved anger is extremely destructive. The sooner you handle your anger, the better.

⑨ **Seek help:** If your anger persists or is out of control, get help. Talk to a counselor or pastor, and commit yourself to learning to let go.

⑩ **Give it to God:** The ultimate solution to every problem is God. If nothing works and letting go seems impossible, give it to him and let him take care of it. He will never let you down.

Do as many of these as are helpful. Letting go isn't always instantaneous, but it is well worth whatever time it takes. So "get rid of all bitterness, rage, anger, harsh words, and slander, as well as all types of evil behavior. Instead, be kind to each other, tenderhearted, forgiving one another, just as God through Christ has forgiven you."[5]

WORRY

Some people are like turtles—most worries just roll off their backs. Others are like sponges—they soak up worries, and over time they sour. Certain people worry more than others, but we all tend to worry about something. It may be money, safety, our appearance, our performance, friends, family, love, or a thousand other things. Worry accomplishes nothing positive. Solomon said that "worry weighs a person down."[6] Paul J. Meyer wrote, "It is a downward spiral . . . it lets the air out of all you do, draining the fun and excitement from everything."

Worry makes us irritable or impatient or negative. It can keep you up at night or make your stomach ache. It can make it hard to concentrate and make you so forgetful you think you have Alzheimer's. Worry can be so overwhelming that it leads to severe stress, panic attacks, phobias, or a number of other anxiety disorders. It's a terrible habit and an incredible waste of time. The more you worry, the less you accomplish. As Mark Twain wrote, "I am an old man and I have known a great many troubles, but most of them have never happened." In the Sermon on the Mount, Jesus says there are two things we need not worry about: today and tomorrow.[7] In my thinking, that covers just about everything. We don't need to worry about today—God will take care of it. We don't need to worry about tomorrow—it's already in his hands. So let go of all your worries. I wonder if the apostle Peter was reflecting on Jesus' words when he wrote, "Give all your worries and cares to God, for he cares about you."[8]

My good friend Pam Vredevelt has written a practical little book entitled *Letting Go of Worry and Anxiety*, which includes many ways to deal with your worries. Here are four of them:

① **Review the facts:** Focus your attention on what *is*, not on what if. A mind that feeds on the facts is less likely to fall prey to a frenzied imagination that casts illusions as reality.

② **Reconnect with the present:** Many of our worries stem from a tendency to overestimate the probability of a harmful event and to exaggerate its potential negative effect.

③ **Refuse to assume the worst:** A concern is a concern, not a major disaster. A temporary setback is just that, not a permanent failure cast in stone for all eternity. Keep that in mind the next time you start to assume the worst.

④ **Rely on faith:** Let's allow our anxieties to be a reminder to surrender ourselves fully to God in trust and humility. Let's use worry to trigger a prayer.

MATERIAL POSSESSIONS

Most of us have way too much stuff. It clutters our lives, but we still dream of new, more exciting possessions. Many of us collect something—clothes, cars, art, trading cards, music, movies, and on and on. We treasure our special things. Stuff may be attractive, but it rarely satisfies for very long. I frequently feel overwhelmed by all the stuff in my house. The problem isn't just that it seems to grow but that it requires care and repair. It must be stored and organized and protected. It often owns us as much as we own it. We love our stuff, but it is an addictive trap.

Jesus tells us not to "store up treasures here on earth" where nothing lasts. Rather, "store your treasures in heaven" because "wherever your treasure is, there the desires of your heart will also be."⁹ We are like children building sandcastles on the seashore, naively thinking that they are strong and indestructible and the ocean's waves will never touch them. Yet what we build and collect here on earth fades so quickly. The waves come, and our castles collapse and are washed away. Within a few minutes we can't even find the place where our beautiful castle once stood so proudly. Possessions don't last. As Randy Alcorn writes in *The Treasure Principle*, "The more you have, the more you'll leave behind."

Stuff is dangerous. Robert Coles, renowned author and child psychiatrist, wrote, "The most dangerous temptation of all is the temptation of plenty." Stuff numbs us. It makes us fat and greedy and envious. It feeds our self-absorption and promotes selfish ambition. It stifles compassion and undermines community. It nurtures shallowness and tempts our spirit. We all have items we need to let go of—not because they are bad in themselves, but because they consume our mind and heart and spirit, distracting us from what is really important.

Dr. Billy Graham tells the story of a little boy who got his hand stuck inside a very valuable vase. His father patiently tried to help the boy remove his hand, but it wouldn't come out. The father was thinking of breaking the vase when he said, "Now, my son, make one more try. Open your hand, and hold your fingers out straight and then pull." To his astonishment the little fellow said, "Oh no, Father. I couldn't put my fingers out like that, because if I did I would drop my penny."

Dr. Graham finishes his story by saying, "Smile if you will—but thousands of us are like that little boy, so busy holding on to the world's worthless penny that we cannot accept liberation. I beg you to drop that trifle in your heart. Surrender! Let go, and let God have his way in your life."

To let go is to admit you can't control everything. To let go is to leave the past behind you and look to a bright and exciting future. To let go is to recognize that anger rarely gets you what you want. To let go is to give all your worries to him who has power over each today and every tomorrow. To let go is to realize that missionary Jim Elliot was right when he said, "He is no fool who gives what he cannot keep to gain what he cannot lose." To let go is to live life to the fullest.

STEP ❻

REACH OUT

The old man lived by the sea. Each day when the tide went out he would slowly, meticulously walk along the rocky shore. Every once in a while he bent down, picked up a starfish that had been stranded by the retreating ocean and would probably die before the tide returned, and threw it back into the sea. One day a neighbor who had frequently watched the old man called out, "Hey, what are you doing? Don't you know that this beach goes on for hundreds of miles, and thousands of starfish get washed up on it every day? Surely you don't think that throwing a few back is going to matter!"

The old man paused with a smile, then held up the starfish in his hand. "It matters to this one," he said.

Every person matters.

Every person you meet has incredible value. Yet it is so easy to walk by them without any sense of how unique and talented and full of incredible potential they are. All we need to do is reach out, but we hesitate. We don't have the time or the interest or the confidence. We leave it to somebody else. In his book Locking Arms, Stu Weber challenges each of us to step forward: "You be the one to reach out. You be the one to start the conversation. . . . Look people in the eye, learn names, study hearts. And reach out."

Reaching out does much more than impact others: It changes and enriches who you are. There are many ways to reach out; we'll look at six of them.

NOTICE

Life is so full and busy in this experience-as-much-as-you-can world. We skim across the surface of life hardly even noticing the people we pass by.

We have perfected the art of seeing without noticing. In Thornton Wilder's play *Our Town*, Emily cries out, "Oh, Mama, just look at me one minute as though you really saw me. . . . Let's look at each other." In frustration she gives up trying to get people to really notice each other and concludes that we are all just blind to those around us. We frequently have eyes that don't truly see and ears that don't seem to hear. As a result, we don't reach out to those around us who need a little compassion. St. Augustine said that we all need hands to help others, feet to hasten to those in need, eyes to see misery and want, and ears to hear the sighs and sorrows of those around us.

I once visited a church that was mourning the suicide of a bright and beautiful sixteen-year-old girl. The people were in shock, unable to absorb the tragedy of it all. But what was the hardest thing to face was her suicide note. The last lines went something like this: "My struggles felt too big and too hard. I tried my best to cry out for help, but nobody seemed to notice." Over the years those last four words have haunted me: *nobody seemed to notice.*

So please look around and notice. Please don't let the words of that six-teen-year-old refer to you.

WELCOME AND ACCEPT

I love a warm welcome. When it is clear someone is glad to see you, he or she makes you feel wanted. The person smiles and asks you all sorts of questions, actually listening to your answers without interrupting. He or she might even ask you to stay for dinner. Then when you must leave, the host appears genuinely sad that your time together has come to an end. Too often when I call someone or drop by that person's home, I feel as if I've interrupted something and that I'm an intruder. The person wishes to be polite, but he or she doesn't have the time to reach out. With places to go and things to do, it feels as if the person is trying to get rid of me in order to move on with life.

The apostle Peter reminds us to "cheerfully share your home with those who need a meal or a place to stay."[1] Most of us yearn for a slower pace where we can really connect with others, but we don't do anything to foster such a world. We don't have the time for hospitality, even though our soul aches for it. Hospitality requires breaking through the tendencies of isolation, detachment, independence, self-protection, and self-absorption. It requires reaching out, and its rewards are incredible. What you gain through hospitality is so much more than what you give. At its core, hospitality means to welcome and accept. Paul put it simply, "Practice hospitality."[2] The Greek word that he uses here encompasses two specific elements: to act as a friend and to act as a host. I encourage you to reach out daily to be both of these. My friend Pastor Doug Hiebenthal wrote that hospitality requires

- including others in your plans and activities;

- setting time aside to make connections with new people;

- making room for people at your table, in your home, and in your life;

- helping people feel included, accepted, and more comfortable;

- sharing what you have with others;

- moving beyond your present friends to include new friends;

- being purposeful in your use of time with others outside your comfort zone;

- responding to others by design and not default.

Integrating these values into your life will enrich you in surprising ways. The writer of Hebrews says, "Don't forget to show hospitality to strangers, for some who have done this have entertained angels without realizing it!"[3]

To welcome others involves accepting them. You need not agree with them or be attracted to them, but you can still reach out and accept them. Paul tells us to "accept one another."[4] Why? Because Jesus accepted you.

LISTEN

King Solomon said, "Let the wise listen and add to their learning."[5] It is amazing how much we can learn by keeping quiet and listening. It is also one of the most effective ways to reach out to others. Paul Tournier writes in *To Understand Each Other* that it is impossible to overemphasize the immense need people have to be really listened to. It affirms them. It shows we care and exhibits respect. Sometimes a silent mouth and an attentive ear is the most loving thing we can offer.

In the middle of the Civil War, Abraham Lincoln was under incredible pressure. There were many who thought he should issue a proclamation to free the slaves. There were others who were furious that he would even consider such a proclamation. Lincoln wasn't sure what to do. He wrote an old friend back in Springfield and asked him to come to the White House. The friend rushed to Lincoln's side and listened as the president talked for hours of the arguments for and against freeing the slaves. He explained the options, read articles, quoted opinions, spoke of consequences, and described feelings. The friend kept listening. Hours later, Lincoln thanked him for all his help, and the good friend traveled back to Springfield. During the hours he had spent with Lincoln, the friend had never said a word. What Lincoln needed most at this critical time was for someone to truly listen.

Everybody wants to be heard. Sometimes just by listening to someone you can help that person

- clarify thinking;
- reduce stress;
- build confidence;
- experience hope;
- feel love.

Listening takes discipline as you stop what you're doing and focus on the other person's words, meanings, emotions, and concerns. Listening says, "You are important." It reaches out by taking an interest in someone else's journey and wanting to know his or her story. When you place your focus on others instead of yourself, your worries and difficulties seem to shrink. Listening builds your character.

UNDERSTAND

Listening with both your mind and heart is the first step to understanding. Let your mind grasp the details of another person's situation and let your heart feel what he or she might be experiencing. It's impossible to fully understand a person because you haven't walked in his or her shoes. Yet you can try, and in so doing you are drawn closer, seeing things through the other's eyes, which involves filtering life through his or her past experiences, current realities, and future dreams. Understanding is hard; it involves setting aside your perspectives and prejudices. It also involves celebrating the other person's joys and weeping with his or her sorrows. It might even involve carrying another's burdens.

Understanding means going below the surface. It accepts that we all have strengths and weaknesses, but it recognizes that these don't make a person good or bad. It watches for similarities and knows that differences make relationships more intriguing. Understanding does not allow differences to create distance but embraces them as keys to our uniqueness. Differences can enrich our lives in many ways. I love to see two people with different personalities learn to understand and appreciate each other. Opposites can be frustrating, but they can also provide great opportunities for growth. Opposite ideas frequently create a balance that protects two people from being too extreme. I am friends with two men, George and Tom, who are on a board that distributes money for a charity. George is very rule-based and follows the very letter of the law, allowing no exceptions. Tom is compassionate. He is known as a "softy," often being overly generous whenever he hears a heartbreaking tale of someone in need.

When they first met, George saw Tom as financially irresponsible and easily manipulated. Tom saw George as hard-hearted and cold. In some ways, both men were correct in their assumptions about the other, but as the years went by, they developed a mutual respect and a realization that they needed each other. Now George asks Tom if he's being too rigid, and Tom discusses policies and procedures for giving with George.

In many marriages or friendships, I often see everyday differences become the source of conflict. One might be an extrovert who wants to spend all his time with people, while his wife is an introvert who cherishes her time alone. Together they discover the importance of public as well as private time.

Money is also a source of conflict in many marriages. If one person is a spender, he has a difficult time sticking to a budget, often spending an entire paycheck before any bills are even paid. On the other hand, if a person is a saver, she runs the risk of getting so wrapped up in not spending that she doesn't enjoy life and often misses opportunities for joy. Together, these two personalities can learn the value of both spending and saving.

With positive communication and genuine understanding, we can learn to strike a balance when we're faced with someone who seems to be our opposite. Most differences are both beneficial and dangerous, depending on what we do with them. The balance is important because it allows us to increase the benefits and decrease the dangers of opposite extremes.

Each of these examples illustrates how we can stretch ourselves and rejoice in the variety of life. Understanding personality differences helps us to avoid conflict and tension. Understanding others helps you to appreciate their uniqueness and helps them to feel they are not quite so alone.

ENCOURAGE AND AFFIRM

Life can be hard. Some days we feel lonely, frustrated, worn-out, rejected, used, depressed, unappreciated, or hopeless. These are the times we need someone to reach out and come alongside us. Billy Graham wrote, "There are so many hurts that circumstances and the world inflict upon us, we need the constant reinforcement of encouragement." Chuck Swindoll simply says, "Man's highest duty is to encourage others."

A good friend of mine was at the grocery store when she felt God nudge her to buy two bouquets of bright spring flowers. So she got one for herself and one to encourage someone else. On the way out of the store, she saw an elderly woman who appeared distraught. My friend walked up to her, handed her a bouquet, and said, "This is for you. Have a great day." A smile crossed the woman's face as she replied, "Oh, thank you. Today is my wedding anniversary, but my husband has passed away. He always gave me flowers on this day." My friend had no idea how encouraging her little gift was going to be.

A little encouragement can make a big difference in a person's life. We all need encouragement. In fact, the great American philosopher and psychologist William James insisted that "the deepest principle of human nature is the craving to be appreciated." Yet the world is full of discouragers. It is easier to ignore, criticize, control, or lecture than it is to reach out and encourage. Discouragement focuses on the negative, while encouragement builds up the positive.

As a psychologist, I've observed over and over again that people become what you encourage them to be. I challenge you to expose people's strengths and cover their weaknesses. Be liberal with your praise. Tell them, "Thank you," "You are great," "You did a fantastic job," and "I really appreciate you." Mother Teresa said, "Kind words can be short and easy to speak, but their echoes are truly endless." The apostle Paul sums it up nicely: "So encourage each other and build each other up."[6]

PRAY

Prayer is an incredible tool. It involves bringing people before God and asking him to provide protection, direction, and blessings. Dick Eastman said, "Prayer reaches out in love to a dying world and says 'I care.'" I used to pray quietly for people without ever letting them know what I was doing. Now I'm more bold about it and I ask, "May I pray for you?" "What do I need to know that would help me pray best for you?" or "Would you like to pray together?" As I've asked these questions, not one person has been offended or turned down my offer of prayer.

When I pray for people, I like to pray for all the areas that make a balanced life. I pray for their

- mind—that they may think clearly and make good, healthy decisions;

- heart—that they know peace and not be overwhelmed by anger, anxiety, or depression;

- relationships—that they reach out and live in harmony with all people;

- body—that they enjoy good health and be kept safe;

- spirit—that they will know God, trust him, and draw near to him.

As I pray I'm reminded of the apostle Paul's words: "So we keep on praying for you, asking God to enable you to live a life worthy of his call.

May he give you the power to accomplish all the good things your faith prompts you to do."[7]

Reaching out frequently means taking a risk. So I'd like to encourage you to pray for people who may be outside your comfort zone. Pray for the weak and disconnected—the minorities, the challenged, the lonely, the hurting, and the struggling people of your world. Pray for your enemies—those who hurt you or hate you or harm you; those who anger you or disgust you or cause you to feel uncomfortable. Pray for the lost and confused—those who are thirsty for love and acceptance, security and recognition. They are like us in more ways than we really wish to admit.

Pray for the people on the fringes—the person who delivers your mail, works at your local gas station, checks your groceries, picks up your garbage, and all the others who live in the shadows of your life. Pray for the strangers—those you don't know and have never met; someone you've heard about or read about; a friend of a friend; a neighbor; anyone new to reach out to. As you reach out to pray for individuals in each of these categories, remember the words of Samuel Taylor Coleridge: "He prayeth best who loveth best."

All six of these means of reaching out are forms of love. In love we give our time and attention, our encouragement and prayers. Ruth Stafford Peale said it so simply: "Find a need and fill it." The world is full of those with needs, both great and small. As you reach out and attempt to meet some of those needs, you can be assured that you are changing your own world in a positive way. Winston Churchill said, "You make a living by what you get. . . . But you make a life by what you give." How beautiful and inspiring to hear stories of people giving to each other. Reaching out is an act of giving—we give patience, respect, and grace. Reaching out must be more than an activity or a hobby or a good deed. It must be an act of giving yourself and an act of love. The apostle Paul gives us all an in-your-face challenge: "Let love be your highest goal!"[8]

Every year thousands of people from all over the world come together for the Special Olympics. It is an exciting event where disabled athletes give their best in joyful competition of sports and determination. A number of years ago, five young runners stood at the starting line. They crouched into position, and the starter's gun fired. The five burst onto the track and were running with all they could give. It was a close race, with each athlete pushing to his limit and the crowd cheering them on.

Suddenly one of the runners tripped and fell flat on his face. He tried to pull himself to his feet, but he was dazed since the wind had been knocked out of him. The crowd gasped, and some shook their heads in sadness, knowing the disappointment of the young runner. But in the next moment a surprise overtook the crowd. Another child stopped running, went back, and reached out to help the fallen boy to his feet. The two of them finished the race together, and the people stood to their feet, cheering them on.

That is love. That is what reaching out is all about.

STEP ❼
CELEBRATE

Joyce felt like a modern-day Job.

In the past year, her husband of twenty-five years had died of a sudden heart attack, she had lost her job because of downsizing, her teenage daughter had gotten into a serious car accident, and now her house was going into foreclosure because she couldn't make the payments. Joyce sat in my office and wept. I wept with her. I wondered, *How can I encourage this woman when her situation seems so overwhelming?*

But then Joyce surprised me. She wiped her tears and said, "Life is hard, but God is good."

"Excuse me?" I said.

"Life is hard," she repeated. "But God is good. I know that somehow he's going to take care of me and the kids. I just want to celebrate that my daughter is alive and that I am healthy and that I have met some of the most wonderful, supportive people ever during the past year."

Celebrate? My mind reeled. *Did she just say celebrate? How can a woman in her situation celebrate?*

After she left, I was struck with the following statement from the beginning of the book of James: "When trouble comes your way, consider it an opportunity for great joy."[1] The prophet Habakkuk paints a vivid illustration of this principle: "Even though the fig trees have no blossoms, and there are no grapes on the vines; even though the olive crop fails, and the fields lie empty and barren; even though the flocks die in the fields, and the cattle barns are empty, yet I will rejoice in the Lord!"[2]

We all need to celebrate in both good times and bad. Some people find joy easy to grasp. They naturally celebrate every opportunity they get. Others find it as elusive as the pot of gold at the end of a rainbow. They feel that joy has been hidden, and no matter how long they look, it stays beyond their grasp.

Medical conditions, depression, loss, anxiety, and failure are just a few of the things that can make joy seem so distant. Yet regardless of how elusive it is, "A cheerful heart is good medicine."[3] It decreases our blood pressure, boosts our immune system, and makes us feel better. It enriches our perspective on life, energizes our spirit, and gives us fulfillment. So we must take celebration seriously. How can we embrace joy?

Choose it: Make a choice about how you think, talk, and act. Be intentional about noticing and focusing on the joy around you.

Pursue it: Chase after joy; be persistent in your journey to find it no matter where it is. Be determined to overcome whatever obstacles might slow you down.

Request it: Jesus said, "Keep on asking, and you will receive what you ask for."[4] Sometimes we don't get something because we haven't asked God for our heart's desire. He is anxious to give us what is good for us, and joy is definitely good for us.

Someone once said that "cheerfulness greases the axles of the world." It energizes us and brightens up our world. It makes us want to dance and celebrate. Life is full of things that make us want to leap for joy. No healthy person would deny the power of love. Literature, movies, and music are full of romantic images. Love makes us want to celebrate. After more than twenty years of marriage to my wife, Tami, I'm still filled with an indescribable joy when I hear a special song or feel her gentle kiss.

It's the same type of feeling I get when I remember the day each of our children was born. The first cry, the tiny hands and feet, the helpless dependency, the incredible potential—these miraculous moments are imprinted on my soul and give me unlimited appreciation for life.

Every day you are surrounded with hundreds of these reasons to celebrate. To live an abundant life you must let these joys fill your heart. To live an abundant life, you must be constantly aware of joy and nurture that joy daily. Rejoice in the intricacies of a spider web, applaud the courage of a child learning to walk, feel the thrill of a well-run race, delight in the words that perfectly capture the moment. As you rejoice in these little things, you will show the world the amazing strength of simple celebration. Let's look at five expressions of joy.

SMILE

An old Japanese proverb says, "Fortune comes to those who smile." In fact, Charles Schwab, the first president of U.S. Steel, once said that his smile was worth a million dollars. We are drawn to people who smile. They make us feel relaxed and accepted. I want to spend time with people who smile because they bring out the smile in me. Dale Carnegie writes in his classic *How to Win Friends and Influence People* that "a smile says, 'I like you. You make me happy. I am glad to see you.'"

A simple smile has great power. I was walking down the sidewalk on a sunny spring morning when I passed a grumpy-looking woman. I was smiling, and I gave her a friendly nod. "Excuse me," she said, "why are you smiling?" I stopped and responded, "It's such a beautiful morning that I can't stop myself." The lady thought about that for a moment and said, "I think I like you." As she walked away, a slight smile began to cross her face.

A smile is a wonderful gift to give others and yourself. So greet anybody you meet with a warm smile. Frank Fletcher once wrote that a simple smile "is rest to the weary, daylight to the discouraged, sunshine to the sad, and nature's best antidote for trouble." Joseph Addison, the English poet, explained the same thought by saying, "What sunshine is to flowers, smiles are to humanity. These are but trifles, to be sure; but, scattered along life's pathway, the good they do is inconceivable." But not only does a smile do good to others, it does good to you. It improves your attitude, it lifts your spirit, and it makes you feel good. No matter what your situation, if you smile, it helps you feel better. And if anyone else sees it, they feel better too. King Solomon sums this up by simply saying, "A cheerful look brings joy to the heart."[5]

LAUGH

I love to laugh. While flying home from Orlando with my family, something in the in-flight movie got me to laugh. This was not your normal calm, controlled laugh. This was a laugh-until-your-sides-ache-and-tears-run-down-your-face sort of laugh. I tried to stop, but it was hopeless. Brittany, my teenage daughter, said, "Dad, it's not that funny."

Through my tears I said, "But everybody else is laughing."

"But can't you see?" she asked. "Nobody is watching the screen. They are all watching you."

There is something freeing about laughter, something that makes all of life seem more joyful. An old French saying insists that "the most completely lost of all days is the one in which I have not laughed." A smile touches your heart, but a laugh touches your whole body. I feel sad for the person who doesn't laugh frequently. To lose the power to laugh is to lose the power to enjoy life. So laugh every chance you get and share your laughter with others. As Thomas Moore prayed, "Lord, give me a sense of humor that I may take some happiness from this life and share it with others."

Healthy people laugh. They have learned the great benefits of letting laughter flow. Here are a few of those benefits:

- **It is contagious:** When you laugh, so do others.

- **It blocks depression:** It is hard to laugh and be depressed simultaneously.

- **It reduces stress:** A good laugh distracts you from your worries.

- **It attracts others:** People are drawn to a hearty laugh.

- **It makes difficult situations tolerable:** A laugh lightens even the heaviest load.

Find something funny and allow yourself a good, long laugh. For as Tim Hansel wrote, "He who laughs . . . lasts."

PLAY

My two sons are constantly asking me, "Dad will you play with us?" They love to play Legos, soccer, basketball, video games, and army men. It's easy to come up with great excuses not to play. There are chores to do and places to go. I'm too tired, too busy, too mature. But what if play is the most important thing you do all day? Children know how to play and have fun;

they smile and laugh and have a great time. Adults should follow their example a little more often. Antoine de Saint-Exupery wrote, "All adults were once children—although few of them remember it." We get too distracted by the serious side of life. We need to develop a playfulness that holds its own against all the cares and concerns that overwhelm us.

Play helps us to lighten up. It relaxes us and brings us joy. Let me share eight "don'ts" to good play I've discovered:

① Don't try to be perfect.
② Don't compare yourself to others.
③ Don't be overly sensitive.
④ Don't take yourself too seriously.
⑤ Don't expect to please everybody.
⑥ Don't be surprised when things go wrong.
⑦ Don't expect to win.
⑧ Don't forget to have fun.

Please don't let these distract you from your joy. Without play we all become grumpy old killjoys who stifle our own ability to have fun and freedom. We become worn-out control freaks who make others uptight and fearful. Therefore, when friends or children or anybody else asks you to play, welcome the opportunity.

GET EXCITED

Life is full of excitement, and this excitement should be celebrated. We fail to let the joy of life touch our emotions and get us energized and enthusiastic. We let ourselves become subdued and bored; we tiptoe through life without diving in and celebrating how amazing it all is. I want to get excited about every sunrise or sunset I view, every breath I take, every person I meet, and every challenge I encounter!

If I allow myself this type of excitement, my joy becomes unstoppable.

I enjoy passionate people—those who have discovered a passion and are enthusiastic about it. If you struggle in this area, commit yourself to *find your passion.* Ask yourself questions such as: *What energizes me? What do I do well? What am I drawn to when I'm bored?* These questions get you started on an amazing journey. A passion is different for each person. For one, it might be an athletic activity; for another, it's working with kids or gardening or writing. Once you think you have found it, *feed your passion*. Explore it, practice it, research it. Spend time and energy developing it. A passion that is not fed can easily wither and die. Lastly I encourage you to *fulfill your passion*. It doesn't have to be your full-time or even part-time job. It may be something you do with your free time. However you fit it into your life, set goals and dreams involving your passions. Goals move you forward, they stretch you, they help you turn your dreams into reality. And a life without dreams is often drained of joys. Dreams add excitement, and excitement leads to celebration.

THROW A PARTY

We all need to throw more parties. Last summer my brothers and sisters and I celebrated our parents' fiftieth wedding anniversary. We planned a big party and had an absolutely wonderful time. Too often we let opportunities for celebration slip by unnoticed. Let's make sure we throw parties for

- birthdays
- weddings
- anniversaries
- births
- holidays
- achievements
- graduations
- appreciation
- engagements
- leaving or coming home

Maybe the best reason to throw a party is because God has been good in one way or another. We might throw one to celebrate the seasons:

winter, spring, summer, or fall. Or maybe we don't even need a reason to throw a party. We can be like the Mad Hatter in *Alice in Wonderland*, who threw a tea party to celebrate his "unbirthday." I just asked my son Dylan for a good reason to throw a party, and he said, "Why not just for fun?" I love that. Let's celebrate and throw a party just for fun. And when you plan your party, don't forget to invite me.

Life is hard. We are surrounded by difficulties, but we still have plenty of opportunities for celebration. Even if the night is dark, joy will come in the morning. Faith involves believing that there is a reason to celebrate, even when the feelings and circumstances don't point in that direction. As G. K. Chesterton wrote, "Joy is the gigantic secret of the Christian." Yet it must be chosen, pursued, and requested. For some it may come quickly and with little effort. For others the journey is long and the effort exhausting. But whoever you are and wherever you may be, my prayer for you is the same as Paul's: "May the God of hope fill you with all joy and peace."[6]

STEP ❽

DIG DEEP

"You've got to dig deeper."

"But isn't this deep enough?"

"Not yet," Dad said. "Put your weight into it. You can go a little deeper."

I can still remember the sweat rolling off my forehead as I was digging fence-post holes with my father. The ground was hard, and at times we'd hit a rock. I'd get tired, and he'd simply say, "Dig deeper."

Later I found that if your post was too shallow, it would become wobbly and maybe even lean to one side or the other. Yet if the post was set deep enough, it would stand strong and straight.

I think this is also true of people. If we dig deep—search for knowledge and work to broaden our outlook—we will stand strong and straight. This is an important means to gain the abundant life. However, this task is not easy. Rick Warren wrote, "There are no shortcuts to maturity." The ground is often hard, and our muscles grow tired. But if we are persistent, the rewards are great.

If you're willing to dig deep, you must be willing to go beyond your own superficiality. We have all grown shallow. William James wrote that "compared with what we ought to be, we are only half awake. . . . We are making use of only a small part of our possible mental and physical resources. . . . The human individual thus lives far within his limits, he possesses powers of various sorts he habitually fails to use." We skate on the surface of life, racing through experiences without truly experiencing them. We rarely dig deep. As Richard Foster said, "Superficiality is the curse of our age." There are at least five basic principles that will lead us to depth and maturity.

COMMIT YOURSELF TO LEARNING

Learning is open to everyone, regardless of age, wealth, social status, or intelligence. The only requirement is that you be teachable, for learning requires an attitude that says, "I'm a student, and I want to know more." This process is active; you must search for it and work for it. Learning isn't always easy; it challenges you by making you think and feel and sometimes even change. This can be exciting and exhilarating, but it can also be uncomfortable. It questions and convicts. It can cut deeply into your beliefs and prejudices, forcing you to rethink and relearn what you once took for granted. Learning allows you to know more but makes you realize how little you truly understand. It also moves you to action—to apply what you have learned and to reach out with that learning to those around you.

I recently met a delightful couple in their mideighties. They were intelligent, articulate, and had an insatiable curiosity. We had a wonderful discussion about everything from current events to geography, theology, movies, and engineering. After a while I asked, "What is your secret to such great conversation?" The wife laughed and said, "It's simple; we are lifelong learners. We are students at the university." He added, "Learning keeps the mind awake." Lifelong learning is a key to growth for there is always more to learn. Harvey Ullman wrote that "anyone who stops learning is old, whether this happens at twenty or eighty." Likewise, digging deep and being lifelong learners keeps you young even if you are eighty-six or older.

READ WIDELY

The world is full of incredible ideas, mind-expanding thoughts, and interesting experiences. Reading opens you up to all these. In their enjoyable little book *God Is in the Small Stuff*, Bruce and Stan write, "Reading is the gateway for growth. Books contain information, insight and inspiration—all of which contribute significantly to your mental and spiritual development. . . . Good books also present ideas and concepts that stretch beyond our self-imposed limits." Therefore dig deep by reading a broad diversity of books, authors, and topics. Try to avoid the trap of reading only those books that reinforce what you already believe.

I love lists. Over the years I have collected a number of book lists, such as The 100 Best Books of All Time, The Most Influential Books of the

Twentieth Century, and The Books That Every Christian Should Read. I want to read books that have had a significant impact on others. In *A Severe Mercy*, Sheldon Vanauken relates an agreement between him and his wife that if either one found a book to be meaningful, the other would read it too. By so doing, they drew closer and discovered a faith that changed their lives.

Finding good and powerful books can be a challenge, but thousands exist. Every time I visit with my brother-in-law, Todd, he will ask me sometime in our conversation, "What good books have you read lately?" If I give him a title, he will pull out a piece of paper from his wallet and write it down. Todd knows the importance of reading widely.

One of the biggest challenges I face is to remember all the wonderful things I've read. If I could only remember it all, I would be brilliant. Kyle Liedtke wrote a few basic principles that can help us retain more of what we read:

- **Highlight** meaningful quotes and impacting principles.

- **Write** the most meaningful ideas in a journal and review them from time to time.

- **Ask** yourself questions like, What is the author's purpose in writing this book? What is the key idea of the book? How can this book help me in my life?

- **Think** about what you read. As one old sage said, "It is better to master ten books than just read one thousand."

- **Speak** with friends about some of the principles you've learned and how they have affected you.

Let me add to Liedtke's principles the importance of rethinking what you've read. This involves studying, reflecting, pondering, and maybe even rereading. Henry David Thoreau summed up this principle by writing, "As a single footstep will not make a path on the earth, so a single thought will not make a pathway in the mind. To make a deep physical path, we walk again and again. To make a deep mental path, we must think over and over the kind of thoughts we wish to dominate our lives."

ASK QUESTIONS

When our kids were preschoolers they asked Tami and me thousands of questions. They constantly asked, "Why?" *Why is the sky blue? Why is water wet? Why do cats have four legs but chickens have only two?* I must admit that at times their questions nearly drove us crazy, but this is how children learn.

Bill Mowry wrote, "Learners ask good questions. They possess an insatiable curiosity—a longing to know, discover, and inquire." You cannot dig deep without asking questions. Yet many people are hesitant to ask. Maybe they believe they should already know the answers, or they are afraid they might sound foolish. Others don't want to pry or interrupt. So they keep their questions locked away, missing real opportunities to learn and dig deep. The solution is simple—just ask. There is nothing wrong, foolish, or inappropriate about an honest question born out of pure motives.

Questions are amazing tools that allow us to get to the heart of an issue or a person. In journalism classes they teach that the basic questions are *Who? What? Where? When? How?* and *Why?* As a psychologist, I ask hundreds of questions of every client I meet. People are usually surprised at how much they open up and what they share in fifty minutes of therapy. But I just ask and listen. The power of a simple question is something we all need to explore.

Questions can

- open up new doors;

- lead to understanding;

- break through superficiality;

- clarify confusion;

- communicate caring;

- correct misinformation;

- reinforce possibilities;

- satisfy curiosity.

Questions are crucial to your growth and ability to dig deep. So ask questions of yourself and others. Everyone you meet—whether a close friend, a complete stranger, or anyone in-between—be prepared with a few questions. Once you get started, who knows where you might end up.

EXPLORE NEW IDEAS

Robin Williams played the innovative teacher John Keating in the movie *Dead Poets Society*. His motto is *carpe diem*, meaning "seize the day." At one point, to the astonishment of his pupils, he jumps onto his desk and proclaims, "I stand upon my desk to remind myself that we must constantly look at things in a different way."

I think John Keating was right. Periodically we all need to study and try to understand different points of view, even if they contradict our perspective. It's healthy to explore new ideas and consider other opinions. Even Solomon wrote: "Intelligent people are always open to new ideas. In fact, they look for them."[1]

Too often we get stuck in the rut of what is comfortable and familiar. New thoughts might force us to reconsider our beliefs and prejudices, and that is far too threatening. So we close our mind and thus stop growing. Will Henry said that "an open mind collects more riches than an open purse." A closed mind collects nothing and often goes bankrupt. An open mind is alive and flexible and capable of seeing any situation from a multitude of perspectives. It has the freedom to rethink its positions and reevaluate its opinions. William Blake wrote that "the man who never alters his opinion is like standing water and breeds reptiles of the mind." I wonder if a lot of us have grown stagnant and need some fresh ideas to clean out our thinking. So what gets us so stuck? Why don't we grow? Here are a few reasons:

- We have a lot to unlearn.
- We are too comfortable.
- We are afraid.
- We don't want to upset people.
- We are easily distracted.
- We are too overwhelmed.

To dig deep is to grow in spite of any of these reasons. It's to face the new with excitement and not let our preconceived notions imprison us. It's to realize that we might not know the answer to every question and to understand that the answers we have held onto so firmly might be incomplete, inaccurate, or imperfect. So I awake each morning wondering what I will discover today. I love the way Samuel Jackson put it: "The world is not yet exhausted; let me see something tomorrow which I never saw before."

SEEK COUNSEL

You can't dig deep without the help of others. We all need a guide—someone who has gone before and knows the way. Someone who is committed to learning can direct us to good books, assist us with probing questions, and present new ideas. Sometimes parents or pastors can fill this role. Other times we need a mentor, coach, spiritual director, counselor, or a group. King Solomon was considered the wisest person in the world, but throughout Proverbs he writes that the key to his success is seeking counsel. He says things like, "Fools think their own way is right, but the wise listen to others." "Walk with the wise and become wise." "Get all the advice and instruction you can, so you will be wise the rest of your life." "Plans succeed through good counsel."[2] If King Solomon needed counsel, the rest of us really need it.

We all need to connect regularly with some type of coach. Yet we often see this as unnecessary or a sign of weakness. We think we can do it on our own, and maybe we can, but why not learn from all who have gone before us? Andy Stanley said, "I can go farther and faster with someone coaching me than I can go alone." I believe this is true of most of us. We all are too close to ourselves and our situations to be objective. We need others to help us work through our blind spots, insecurities, and weaknesses. James Belasco wrote, "Coaches help people grow. They help people see beyond what they are today to what they can become tomorrow." In Gary Collins's valuable book *Christian Coaching*, he shares an extensive list of things a coach can help you do. Here are a few of his ideas:

- Develop skills.

- Discover and develop passions.

- Find a life purpose.

- Build a clearer vision for the future.

- Learn to manage change effectively.

- Learn to relate to people effectively.

- Find clear values.

- Appraise performance.

- Get out of ruts and move forward.

- Build self-confidence.

- Learn to take responsibility.

- Develop a closer walk with God.

Finding a coach starts with looking around you for those people whom you respect—those people who are wise or accomplished or skilled in areas you wish to pursue. In the Scriptures we find Moses mentoring Joshua, Eli teaching Samuel, Elijah being a role model for Elisha, and Paul guiding Timothy. Mentoring can happen formally or informally, individually or in a small group. The key is to be humble, teachable, and determined to become all that God wants you to be.

My grandfather was a great coach. As a kid, I admired how he could do almost anything. He taught me how to tie my shoes, drive a tractor, and pan for gold. One day he grabbed a shovel and a gold pan, and the two of us walked down to the Rough and Ready Creek. He explained that long ago the creek had shifted and left a vein of gold deep in the bank. So he forced his shovel into the sandy soil and reminded me, "You've got to dig deep." After digging awhile, he put some of the sand into my pan, and I dipped it into the creek. Then I swirled the water around and around in the pan until the lighter material was washed away. If I was patient and persistent I would soon see a small streak of glitter at the bottom of my pan.

I learned some important lessons through this process, but the most important was that if you dig deep enough in the right spots and work your pan long enough, you will be amazed at the gold you can find in the most ordinary places.

STEP ❾

WORK HARD

Paralyzed from head to toe.

A massive stroke imprisoned forty-three-year-old Jean-Dominique Bauby inside his own body, leaving him unable to speak or even move. With only his left eye functioning, he was able to communicate by blinking to select letters one at a time as a special alphabet was slowly recited to him. Through hard work, along with discipline and persistence, Jean-Dominique meticulously blinked out over sixteen thousand words to compose an amazing book. In *The Diving Bell and the Butterfly* he artfully tells what's going on inside of him with observations that are both fascinating and emotionally charged.

To write a book is no easy task, but to write in Jean-Dominique's condition must have been incredibly demanding. Yet when the final letter of the final page was communicated, I bet he felt a rush of joy and satisfaction. Finishing a day of hard work feels so rewarding. You feel good, and you know it was somehow all worth it. Margaret Thatcher, former prime minister of Great Britain, wrote, "Look at a day when you are supremely satisfied at the end. It's not a day when you lounge around doing nothing; it's when you've had everything to do, and you've done it."

Many successful people praise the value of hard work. Charles Schwab, the first president of U.S. Steel, stated, "Hard work is the best investment a person can make." In a speech in New York on September 7, 1902, Theodore Roosevelt said, "Far and away the best prize that life offers is the chance to work hard at work worth doing." Horace said, "Life grants nothing without hard work." Solomon wrote, "Those who work hard will prosper."[1] Even the apostle Paul wrote, "Work hard and cheerfully at whatever you do, as though you were working for the Lord rather than for people."[2]

At the end of a day of hard work, whether at the office or outside in my yard, I feel good. Sure I might be tired or my muscles might ache, but I have a feeling of accomplishment. Hard work moves me forward at every potential level—mentally, emotionally, socially, physically, and spiritually—though not always at the same time. Hard work can also keep me out of trouble. As Voltaire writes in *Candide*, "Work saves us from three great evils: boredom, vice, and need." When thinking about why work is so important, there are three challenges we would be wise to consider.

AVOID EXTREMES

Life requires balance in many areas. The old saying about moderation in all things has a lot of merit. Extremes might be exciting, but they are also dangerous. In terms of work, there is the extreme of too little work (laziness) and too much work (drivenness). The goal is hard work—active but not all-consuming; focused but not obsessive; determined but not inflexibly stubborn.

Laziness takes you nowhere. It blocks growth. Unmotivated or half-hearted effort is really no effort at all. Emerson wrote, "Without work one finishes nothing." Laziness traps you in immaturity. A lazy person is rarely successful, respected, or happy. It's interesting how many times Solomon warns about the dangers of laziness. He says, "A lazy person has trouble all through their life" and "The desires of lazy people will be their ruin, for their hands refuse to work."[3]

The opposite side of laziness is drivenness, where work becomes your life. Here are ten characteristics of drivenness:

① You frequently are too busy.
② You are obsessed with your goals.
③ Your identity becomes what you do.
④ You don't have time for people.
⑤ You feel guilty if you aren't busy.
⑥ Your focus is primarily on accomplishments.
⑦ You lose your sense of true priorities.
⑧ Competition and winning affect your attitude.
⑨ You are constantly raising your goals.
⑩ Your stress blocks you from being able to relax, laugh, or have fun.

If you have three or more of the above characteristics, you are probably driven.

Laziness gets you nothing, but drivenness rarely gets you what you
really want. If you work hard, you give 100 percent when you need to
but stop at a reasonable point. I work hard each day helping people with
their struggles, and while driving home I do my best to move my
thoughts away from work. By the time I arrive home, I want my focus to
be on my family.

PRACTICE EXECUTION

Execution is the discipline of getting things done. It involves following a
dream through to reality. Anything that is really worthwhile requires discipline, and discipline is hard work. M. Scott Peck, in *The Road Less Traveled*,
insists that "without discipline we can solve nothing." Discipline gives
our hard work direction. Therefore the book of Proverbs reminds us that
"to learn, you must love discipline."[4] I would add that to grow you must
love discipline.

Execution is like a car, and discipline is fuel that keeps things moving.
Larry Burkett stated that "those who are successful in any field . . . have a
desire to achieve that is coupled with discipline." To execute your goals,
you must demonstrate discipline in each of the following six areas.

① **Plan:** Know where you want to end up. Set clear, specific,
realistic goals. Take the time to think a problem through, do
your research, and consult with others. Without a plan, you
won't reach your goal. Henry Kaiser, founder of Kaiser
Permanente Health Care, says, "Every minute spent planning
will save two in execution."

② **Prepare:** The Boy Scout motto is "Be prepared." Good
preparation can save you time and energy and can protect you
from failure. Plato stated, "Preparation is the most important
part of hard work."

③ **Push:** This is where you roll up your sleeves and do the
necessary tasks. It may be challenging, overwhelming, and
exhausting. That's what hard work is all about. Thomas Edison

said, "Opportunity is missed by most people because it is dressed in overalls and looks like work."

④ **Pace:** Timing can be everything. You must know when to start and when to step back, when to be aggressive and when to be patient. Going too fast can burn you out, while going too slow can cause you to miss out. Pacing requires rhythm and progress. It involves moving forward—sometimes at a slow walk, sometimes at a steady jog, sometimes at a full run. As Conrad Hilton said, "Successful people keep moving."

⑤ **Persist:** It is easy to give up when things get too difficult, aren't going as you thought they would, or don't seem fair. Calvin Coolidge said, "Nothing in the world can take the place of persistence." To persist is to complete what you started. James says that when this quality "is fully developed, you will be perfect and complete, needing nothing."[5]

⑥ **Pay-Off:** We all like a reward or pay-off. It may be as simple as telling ourselves, "Great job." It might involve encouragement from others or a sense that we did the right thing. Doing something special to celebrate the completion of hard work can be a wonderful way to wrap up what you just accomplished. Yet we must also remember the truth behind the following words by John C. Maxwell: "The highest reward for your work is not what you get for it, but what you become by it."

PURSUE EXCELLENCE

We live in a world of mediocrity. Too often we don't take the time or make the effort to do things well. We frequently fall into the trap of thinking that just getting it done is good enough. We have grown used to halfhearted effort. Pearl Buck wrote, "The secret joy in work is contained in one word—excellence. To know how to do something well is to enjoy it." I am not speaking of perfection, which is something none of us will ever achieve. But with excellence we do our very best, given our particular circumstances, whether the job is large or small.

Aiming at excellence is incredibly rewarding, even if we don't hit it. Solomon reminds us, "Whatever you do, do well."[6] I have discovered that excellence

- feels good;

- increases optimism;

- defeats doubt and depression;

- builds confidence;

- deepens character.

Excellence cannot happen without execution of the six areas of discipline mentioned above.

Shake free of mediocrity, and don't accept less than you're capable of. Slow down and do fewer things, but do those things well. Mahatma Gandhi said, "It is the quality of our work which will please God, not the quantity." Martin Luther King Jr. put it this way: "If it falls your lot to be a street sweeper, just go on out and sweep streets like Michelangelo painted pictures, sweep streets like Handel and Beethoven composed music, sweep streets like Shakespeare wrote poetry; sweep streets so well that all the hosts of heaven and earth will have to pause and say, 'Here lived a great street sweeper who swept his job well.'" It is sad that we so often settle for mediocrity when the Lord of the universe can empower us with excellence. Remember that with God all things are possible.

DO YOUR BEST

The admiral never smiled.

He stared without blinking straight into the eyes of the twenty-two-year-old officer. The young man was saturated with cold sweat, but the admiral kept up the interrogation. Question after question for three long hours.

Finally Admiral Rickover, the father of the nuclear navy, asked something the young man felt good about. "How did you stand in your class at the Naval Academy?"

"Sir, I stood 59th in a class of 820."

Instead of offering congratulations, the admiral asked, "Did you do your best?"

Jimmy started to say, "Yes sir," but after a quick reflection he gulped and said, "No sir, I didn't always do my best."

"He looked at me for a long while," Jimmy Carter wrote in his auto-biography, *Why Not the Best?*, "and then turned his chair around to end the interview. He asked one final question, which I have never been able to forget—or to answer. He said, 'Why not?' I sat there for a while, shaken, and then slowly left the room."

Why didn't I work harder or aim higher? Why didn't I finish stronger? These are questions we all must ask ourselves, and each of our answers will be different. But ultimately the most convicting question is the one Jimmy Carter still asks himself: *Why didn't I do my best?*

STEP ⑩

REST

Jon was burned out.

He worked six days a week plus half a day on Sunday. He stayed up late writing reports and frequently fell asleep before he made it to his bed. His alarm clock woke him early, and he started his day so exhausted it took two cups of black coffee before he could keep his eyes open. Jon's life was his work. He was constantly on the go and rarely slowed down. He was successful on the job, but the rest of his life suffered. His marriage fell apart, and his health faltered. He didn't have time for fun, and he didn't know how to relax.

At the age of forty-five, Jon had a breakdown. It started with panic attacks and ended with an inability to concentrate on anything for more than three minutes.

"What can I do?" Jon asked his doctor. "I feel like I'm going crazy."

His doctor looked him square in the eye. "My prescription is simple— rest."

Hard work is important, but it must be balanced with rest. Without rest we grow tired and lose our focus. Our mind becomes dull, our heart anxious, our body listless, our relationships frustrating, and our spirit empty. Life wears us down and depletes our energy. Rest fills us up and reenergizes us. Rest is like an oasis in the midst of a hot and hectic desert. It is cool, calm, and completely refreshing. There is nothing else quite like it. So in this desert called life, which can so easily sap all our strength, here are three types of oases that I can't live a fulfilled life without.

A GOOD NIGHT'S SLEEP

Sleep is one of the most important things we do. It renews, restores, and rejuvenates. This is a tired generation, filled with fatigue and exhaustion.

We are worn-out at every level—mentally, emotionally, physically, socially, and spiritually. As I've spoken to thousands of worn-out people, I'm surprised at how frequently the problem is not getting a good night's sleep. If you ignore this area of your life, you will collapse at each of the five levels—mental, physical, spiritual, in your heart, and in your relationships.

You must have good quality and quantity of sleep. You can't cheat either without paying a high price. There is nothing more wonderful than waking from a restful sleep with the energy and excitement to take on a new, glorious day.

Here are ten suggestions for a restful sleep:

① Sleep six to eight hours per night.
② Get up at the same time each day.
③ Exercise regularly, but not within four hours of bedtime.
④ Don't go to bed angry.
⑤ Unwind and relax in the hour before sleep.
⑥ Avoid caffeine, sugar, and heavy meals shortly before bed.
⑦ Play calming music.
⑧ Make sure your mattress and pillows are comfortable.
⑨ Imagine something positive as you fade off.
⑩ Pray as you prepare for sleep.

With a solid night of restful sleep you awake thinking more clearly with life looking brighter. You also find it easier to reach out to others and to be motivated to draw close to God. Without sleep you are unable to pay attention. James Maas, a specialist in sleep research at Cornell University said: "Good sleep is the best predictor of life span and quality of life."

A RELAXING DAY OFF

Moses tells us, "In six days the Lord made heaven and earth, but on the seventh day he stopped working and was refreshed."[1] We all need to set aside a weekly day of rest. This can be a special day when we don't work or even talk about work. In a busy, frantic, do-as-much-as-you-can world, we desperately need a day set apart to slow down and catch our breath. We are a "doing" people who need a time of simply "being." We are surrounded by constant stimulation, activities, temptations, and opportunities. One day out of seven, we need to stop and say no. So take off your shoes, relax, and stay a while.

Isaiah wrote that God "will make rivers in the dry wasteland so my chosen people can be refreshed."[2] In the Hebrew language the word for *refresh* means "to breathe." As people race so rapidly from place to place, I've noticed that many don't really breathe. They huff and puff and take quick, short breaths, but they don't fill their lungs and breathe deep. To be refreshed you must be intentional. You must choose to take the day off. If you don't, your day of rest will quickly get filled up and soon look like every other hectic day of the week.

A day of rest heals our body and spirit. It renews us. That beautiful psalm of David says, "He lets me rest in green meadows; he leads me beside peaceful streams."[3] And when we follow God, we are given the same promise David was given: "He renews my strength."[4] We all need regular times of renewal, or we will wear out and burn out. C. H. Spurgeon put it this way in a lecture to his students: "Fishermen must mend their nets, and we must, every now and then, repair our mental states and set our machinery in order for future service. It is wisdom to take occasional furloughs. In the long run, we shall do more by sometimes doing less."

A day of rest is a wonderful time for contemplation. Dr. Laura Schlessinger speaks of this as a day that "reconnects you to your ultimate purpose of life" and helps you "to find meaning in the moment." We all need time for contemplation; it's essential for personal spiritual growth. Jo Kadlecek writes in *Feast of Life* that contemplation is "when we really consider our ways, reflect on our motives, or ponder our purpose." Later in her book she writes that contemplation "gives us new ways to see the world, new prayers to pray for others, new understandings about scripture passages we may have read several times before, and new insights to lead us closer to the person God always dreamed we would be."

A set-aside day need not be static or boring. It is a gift to yourself that adds depth to your life. It also allows you to be more effective in the other six days of your week. Here are a few ideas of activities to do on your relaxing day off:

- reading and studying

- playing with friends or family

- walking or hiking

- visiting and talking with others

- attending church

- praying

- writing letters or journaling

- enjoying the beauty of music or nature

BREAKS AND GETAWAYS

We all need to find times and places in which to retreat from the on-slaught of people, noise, and activity that bombards us every day. Even Jesus had to escape the crowds. He would get up early in the cool of the morning to be alone with God. At other times he would ask the disciples to take him to the far side of the lake in their fishing boat. We all need breaks and getaways. These moments might be as simple as five quiet minutes in the early morning or an afternoon walk in a park, or as elaborate as a weekend escape at a retreat center.

These escapes become a sanctuary of tranquility within an overwhelming whirlwind. In this sanctuary of solitude, silence, and stillness, amazing things happen that rarely happen elsewhere:

- Truth is pondered.

- Inspiration is born.

- Visions are cast.

- Character is developed.

- Wrongs are forgiven.

- Peace is embraced.

- Love is nurtured.

- Faith is enlarged.

- Healing is discovered.

- Joy is planted.

The greatest benefit of all is that we can finally hear the voice of God. So as we set up our breaks and getaways we must consider three S terms. *Solitude* conveys the absence of distraction, *silence* is the absence of noise, and *stillness* refers to the absence of activity.

SOLITUDE

In solitude we escape all those things that trap, worry, and oppress us. We get away from others' expectations and judgments. We don't do this out of pride or hostility but to gain perspective—a perspective that teaches us how to love more selflessly and come closer to others with greater understanding. Richard Foster writes in *Celebration of Discipline* that "the fruit of solitude is an increased sensitivity and compassion for others." Solitude helps us handle life with grace and patience. It is not an attempt to exclude oneself from people, but an attempt to reach out and come closer in the healthiest of all ways. As Phillip G. Hamerton reminds us, "We need society, and we need solitude also, as we need summer and winter, day and night, exercise and rest."

Solitude deepens us. Henri Nouwen called it "the furnace of transformation," for what happens in solitude always affects what happens outside it. Oswald Chambers wrote, "Solitude with God repairs the damage done by the fret and noise and clamor of the world." Solitude is a beautiful place where I can close out the negativity and pressures that try to steal my peace. For me, it is my backyard with sunlight filtering through the firs or a sunset at the ocean or an early morning drive to my office. Chuck Swindoll wrote, "Solitude is the cultivation of serenity, a deliberate moving toward peacefulness and contentment, which breeds a sense of security within." Solitude is good company, and it is as close as the next moment or your own backyard.

SILENCE

Noise distracts, annoys, interrupts, entertains, and wounds us. Jochen Schacht stated, "Our ears are not made for a noisy world." Modern life is so loud. We are surrounded by radios, television, telephones, computers, CD players, cell phones, and a thousand other invasive sounds. In fact, we are frequently uncomfortable with silence. We avoid it, fight it, fill it. Yet Mother Teresa said that "God . . . cannot be found in noise and restlessness. God is the friend of silence. See how nature—trees and flowers and grass—grow in silence. See the stars, the moon and the sun, how they move in silence."

Isaiah wrote, "In quietness and confidence is your strength."[5] Embrace silence and surrender yourself to it. In 1577, Teresa of Avila wrote in *The Interior Castle* about "the Prayer of Quiet," where we experience "a sense of spiritual sweetness." Silence is good. It is where we find ourselves and God. It is a place where stress fades and peace grows. In *Meditations on Silence*, Sister Wendy Beckett writes, "Entering into silence is like stepping into cool clear water. The dust and debris are quietly washed away, and we are purified of our triviality. This cleansing takes place whether we are conscious of it or not: The very choice of silence . . . washes away the day's grime." I don't know about you, but there are certainly days when I need the grime washed away.

STILLNESS

As a Boy Scout, I learned that when you've lost your way in the woods, you should stop and stay in one spot. Don't panic. Don't frantically run about. Just be still. Rollo May wrote, "It's an old and ironic habit of the human race to run faster when we have lost our way." Somehow we believe that if we are active and busy, we will discover our direction. Yet we only become more lost, more frantic, more confused. When David was in this predicament he wrote, "I have stilled and quieted myself, just as a small child is quiet with its mother."[6] Once he was still, he could discover his way.

Stillness is an essential part of growing deeper. Pam Vredevelt wrote that "perhaps stillness is a prerequisite for knowing." Stillness is not something we do; it's something we don't do. It sounds easy, but it's not. It takes practice and discipline to develop a stillness of mind, heart, and body. I'm like most people—I hate waiting. I'm impatient. I want something to happen, and I want it to happen now. So when David says, "Wait patiently for the Lord,"[7] I cringe a little. But I know he's right, so I wait and I practice being still. It's a difficult lesson, but movement without wisdom and direction is either wasted or dangerous. Therefore, I wish to follow the council of François Fénelon, a seventeenth-century spiritual advisor: "Learn to wait for God. Do not move until he directs you."

Stillness draws you closer to yourself and God. The psalmist gives us God's perspective: "Be still, and know that I am God."[8] When we embrace solitude while being silent and still, we will receive an amazing awareness of God's presence. As John Baillie writes in *A Diary of Private Prayer*, "All day long have I toiled and striven; but now in the stillness of heart and the clear light of thine eternity, I would ponder the pattern my life is weaving." Stillness opens our eyes and ears to our master's movements. So as T. S. Eliot prayed, "Teach us to sit still."

In the middle of her life, Anne Morrow Lindbergh left her hectic life for a few weeks on the North Atlantic coast. She stayed alone in a secluded beach cottage with no heat, no telephone, no water, no rug, no curtains. She went away to rest and relax and reflect. In the process of getting away, Anne discovered the wonder of life, and she journaled her contemplations in the best-selling *Gift from the Sea*. Here she writes, "It is a difficult lesson to learn today—to . . . deliberately practice the art of solitude for an hour or a day or a week." As she adjusted to her time of rest, she concluded that "every person . . . should be alone sometime during the year, some part of each week, and each day." Anne Morrow Lindbergh learned about rest and in so doing she discovered that life is more than activity and hecticness. Without solitude, silence, or stillness, Anne's getaway would have been just another two-week period on a busy calendar. But instead, it fostered reflections that gave her new meaning. The steps of solitude, silence, and stillness are key in our search for an abundant life. They help us to see vividly, hear clearly, and feel fully God's presence. As you practice these steps, carefully consider where you are headed and what sort of life you would like to be living. Let rest rejuvenate you and give you renewed purpose.

STEP ⑪

CLING TO THE POSITIVES

He was number 119,104.

Viktor Frankl was a psychiatrist. He was also an inmate for three years at Auschwitz and other Nazi concentration camps during World War II. In his book *Man's Search for Meaning,* Dr. Frankl writes about being cold, hungry, naked, and frightened. He was beaten, humiliated, and pushed to the brink of human suffering.

How could a person survive such cruel and horrific conditions? Dr. Frankl writes that the Gestapo could take everything away from you but your attitude. You could choose to cling to the positive. If you did that, there was hope. If you didn't, you were doomed. If you focused on the suffering and gave up, you would soon die. Frankl writes, "Woe to him who saw no more sense in his life, no aim, no purpose, and therefore no point in carrying on. He was soon lost."

Dr. Frankl discovered this amazing truth: If we cling to the positive, we can thrive in the worst of all situations. Yet we are surrounded by negativity—it pushes and pressures us every day. And if we let it into our mind or heart, it will spread like a wildfire until negative thoughts and feelings consume us. Soon we begin scattering sparks of negativity to everyone we meet.

To have a great life we must cling to the positives. Doing so allows us to see clearly, to have the right perspective, and to meet our goals. We can be optimistic because we know God cares about us and is ultimately in control. We need to be realistic about our brokenness, but we can be optimistic because we know that God is willing to heal and forgive. Here are six basic ideas that will move us in that direction.

FLEE NEGATIVITY

Negativity kills. It kills joy and relationships and ideas. It kills enthusiasm and motivation. Ultimately it kills hope. If you expect negativity, it will happen. If you ponder negativity, you will become discouraged. If you dwell in negativity, you will become trapped. If you share negativity, you will drive people away.

I despise negativity because I see how badly it hurts and destroys people. As a psychologist, I frequently work with good, kindhearted people who have allowed negativity to take hold of their lives. Four of the most common ways that negativity takes hold are comparison, perfectionism, downhill thinking, and twisted influences.

Comparison: I wish I could write as well as Max Lucado, be as compassionate as Mother Teresa, and play basketball like Michael Jordan. The more I consider what I don't have or can't do, the less I am able to see what God has given me. In 1927 an obscure lawyer from Indiana, Max Ehrmann, wrote a code for healthy living called "Desiderata." In it he says, "If you compare yourself with others, you may become vain or bitter, for always there will be greater and lesser persons than yourself." When we compare, we focus on our own shortcomings rather than our strengths—and thus breed negativity. The most common areas of comparison is what I call the "six As":

①   Appearance—how we look
②   Articulation—how we speak
③   Attitude—how we think
④   Accomplishments—what we do
⑤   Acquisition—what we have
⑥   Ability—where we excel

Remember, you have unique talents and abilities. Get your eyes off others, and look at what God wants to do with you.

Perfectionism: No one is perfect. We all make mistakes, and we all fail at times. If you aim at the unattainable, you will end up frustrated and defeated. Accept your weaknesses and failures, but at the same time try to do your best. Aim at excellence, not perfection. Mistakes happen, and failures occur. Forgive yourself, and learn from what has happened. If others can't accept your imperfections, they are not being realistic or compassionate. Perfectionism comes from unrealistic expectations about life, others, or yourself. If you aren't perfect, you are human.

Downhill Thinking: Negative thinking will make you negative. As you think, so you will be. Marcus Aurelius believed that "a man's life is what his thoughts make of it." So take charge of your thoughts. To focus on the negative will send your life on a downhill slide.

Don't look for the negative.

Don't expect the negative.

Don't exaggerate the negative.

Don't dwell on the negative.

Ralph Waldo Emerson summed it up by saying, "A man is what he thinks about all day."

Twisted Influences: This world is full of dark and ugly things. Some days I can't stand to watch the news or read the paper because of all the negative influences. The world is full of greed, hate, selfishness, cruelty, immorality, deception, and destruction. There is no longer a sense of right or wrong. The world appears to have lost its moral compass. Presidents lie, corporations cheat, television promotes unfaithfulness, movies constantly push the moral limits. Paul writes to Timothy "that in the last days" people will "consider nothing sacred."[1] We are surrounded by negative influences, and if we aren't careful they will rub off on us.

LOOK FOR POSITIVES IN EVERY SITUATION

Your focus will affect your attitude. If you look for the best, you will find it. So I try to do what the apostle Paul suggests. He says to fix your thoughts on "what is true, and honorable, and right, and pure, and lovely, and admirable. Think about things that are excellent and worthy of praise."[2]

These eight things provide a positive focus. They help build attitudes that can rise above all the negative influences of this world. To focus on the negative gives it power; but to focus on the positive gives you power. Martha Washington wrote, "I've learned from experience that the greater part of our happiness or misery depends on our dispositions and not our circumstances."

You can miss the best things in life if you have the wrong attitude. In *Dream a New Dream*, Dale Galloway writes that your attitude can

- make you or break you;

- heal you or hurt you;

- make you friends or make you enemies;

- put you uptight or put you at ease;

- make you miserable or make you happy;

- make you a failure or make you an achiever.

Holding on to a positive attitude can make all the difference in the world. You are in charge of your attitude. Steer in the right direction, and you might be surprised at what might come about. As Dr. Robert Schuller says, "When it's dark, look for the stars."

I want to be an optimist—one who sees the best and believes the best. Winston Churchill declared that "an optimist sees the opportunity in every difficulty." They do not give up. He or she is excited and challenged by the amazing possibilities which rest in almost every situtaion. A healthy optimist is neither naive, unrealistic, or blind. He or she simply sees beyond the limits and challenges which absorb the focus of most people. Optimism is a choice that sheds positive light wherever you may go. A positive attitude tends to make your optimism come true. And the longer and stronger you hold on to it, the better you feel and the brighter the world around you appears. Helen Keller, though blind and deaf, was a delightful optimist. She wrote, "No pessimist ever discovered the secret of the stars or sailed to an uncharted land or opened a new doorway for the human spirit."

FILL YOUR LIFE WITH POSITIVES

I love positive people. They energize and excite me. Negative people wear me out. Complainers and discouragers frustrate me and, over time, sap my energy. In fact, negative people can make me negative. So when I'm feeling down, I want to stand close to an optimist and soak in his or her sunshine. Just as I am drawn to positive people, so are others. Therefore, I want to be someone who energizes and encourages others. I want to be an optimist who can pull others out of the mud and grime of this world.

When I feel stressed or overwhelmed, I yearn for a positive setting—a park, a beach, a forest, a garden. These are positive places for me, where the beauty and peacefulness of nature can calm my spirit. A positive atmosphere can refresh me in amazing ways. The sound of water, a warm breeze, a peaceful landscape, or a multicolored sunset are just a few of the positive places that bring me joy.

Certain other things clear my mind and fill me with positive feelings:

- good books

- peaceful music

- delightful movies

- warm memories

- relaxing baths

- favorite desserts

These positive things allow me to wash all the negatives out of my mind. Yet the most effective means of filling your life with positives is to think beyond this world. The apostle Paul writes, "Think about the things of heaven."[3] For no matter how dark or ugly or negative this world may get, God can give you hope. Knowing that he loves us, forgives us, and has a great dream for us can have an incredibly positive effect on our life. Thomas Moore wrote that "earth has no sorrow that heaven cannot heal."

PRACTICE POSITIVES

Negativity comes naturally, but positives take practice. It is easy to be selfish, greedy, and insensitive. But Paul reminds us, "A man reaps what he sows."[4] If you sow negativity, you will reap negativity. Yet if you sow positives, you will reap positives. So "turn from evil and do good."[5] Set your sights on key virtues that you will proactively build into your life. Here is my list:

- honesty

- respect

- courage

- self-discipline

- kindness

- compassion

- patience

- humility

- God-centeredness

- fairness

- generosity

- obedience

- purity

- responsibility

I am sure there are more positives which I could practice, but these fourteen provide me with a lifetime of challenges.

Just as it is important to practice positives in all you do, it is equally important to practice positives in all you say. In his letter to the church in Ephesus, Paul says, "Let everything you say be good and helpful, so that your words will be an encouragement to those who hear them."[6] Positive words are incredibly powerful. They can bring joy and hope and healing to those around you. Simple words like "Thank you," "Good job," "I appreciate you so much," "I love you," "Fantastic," or "You are wonderful" can make a world of a difference. As Ella Wheeler Wilcox said, "Talk happiness. The world is sad enough without your woe."

REPLACE EVERY NEGATIVE WITH A POSITIVE

No matter how hard you try, sooner or later negativity will try to pull you down. But you can fight it and change your attitude. In his international best seller, *The Power of Positive Thinking*, Norman Vincent Peale writes, "Whenever a negative thought . . . comes to mind, deliberately voice a positive thought to cancel it out." We all have negative, unhealthy, and hurtful thoughts from time to time. When they come, we can either invite them to stay or kick them out. But if we kick them out and don't replace them, the negative will return. Dr. Peale uses three positive affirmations to keep the negatives from returning. He says to himself, *God is with me; God is helping me; God is guiding me.* Many people use positive affirmations to keep the door to their mind secure from unwelcome intruders.

Yet too often we are our own worst enemies. We tell ourselves that we can't do it or we have failed or we are stupid. We give up or get angry. Our negative self-talk can be our defeat. So we must choose to replace it with positive self-talk. I believe the best positive affirmations come directly from the Bible. Here are ten affirmations I suggest you use often so that they become a natural part of your self-talk:

①   This is the day the Lord has made. We will rejoice and be glad in it.

②   My purpose is to give them a rich and satisfying life.

③   I am leaving you with a gift—peace of mind and heart.

④   With God all things are possible.

⑤   If God is for us, who can ever be against us?

⑥   Come to me, all of you who are weary and carry heavy burdens, and I will give you rest.

⑦   Nothing in all creation will ever be able to separate us from the love of God.

⑧   And be sure of this: I am with you always.

⑨   The Lord your God . . . will neither fail you nor abandon you.

⑩   For I can do everything through Christ, who gives me strength.[7]

These positive affirmations can become the basis of positive thinking. So use them throughout the day whenever a negative thought pops up. As Mike Huckabee, the governor of Arkansas, reminds us, "Positive thinking is powerful medicine." It can heal the worst negative.

BE THANKFUL

Being thankful keeps you focused on the positive. While dwelling on what you are thankful for, it is difficult to be negative. Charlie "Tremendous" Jones claimed that "learning to be thankful covers it all." Every day I try to review at least a few of the things I'm thankful for. Today at different times, I've thanked God for my three kids, sunshine, a tall glass of water, friends, health, and my wife. The book of Psalms says, "Give thanks to the Lord, for he is good!"[8] Julian of Norwich reminds us that "thanksgiving is a blessed thing in his sight."

Thankfulness leads to optimism, which overflows into hope and joy. Gratitude reminds us of all we have. It causes us to embrace life with a sense of excitement and expectation. It brings us to a point of appreciation and celebration.

Ingratitude is a denial of reality and the goodness of God. It is greedy (wanting more) and blind (unable to see all that it has). As we cling to the positives, we will become more and more thankful. Erwin McManus writes in *Uprising*, "When we are grateful, we are more fully alive. Gratitude allows us to absorb every possible pleasure from a moment. When your heart is full of gratitude, life paints itself in far brighter and more vivid colors."

If we stop and think about it, we all have a lot to be thankful for. M. R. Vincent wrote that "the Christian is suspended between blessings received and blessings hoped for, so he should always give thanks." The world is full of blessings. Even failures, difficulties, and disappointments can actually be blessings. We often feel thankful only if things go our way. But I believe we can and should be thankful regardless of what happens.

The difficulty in being thankful is really a crisis of creativity. We take so much for granted that our eyes grow old. We don't recognize the incredible things that surround us each day. If we would only stop and look around, we would see a multitude of things for which to be thankful. An ancient prayer spoke of this: "For all thy blessings known and unknown, remembered and forgotten, we give thee thanks." Anne Lamott's book *Traveling Mercies* recounts the joys and sorrows of her life. Her journey has not been an easy one, and yet she ends her book with a bold statement of "Thank you. Thank you. Thank you." Maybe that's the way we should end every day, every conversation, every task.

By the time the boy was thirteen, he was legally blind. His father beat him when he ran into doors or misplaced tools, telling him that all he was good for was selling pencils on a street corner. Then life got harder. He had two bouts of what was diagnosed as terminal cancer and multiple surgeries to remove twelve tumors on his spine, which left him in chronic pain. Yet all who know him shake their heads in amazement, saying it's almost impossible to find a man more content than Bill Van Atta.

Bill chose to cling to positives. He worked his way through school, passed the bar exam, and is now a lawyer in Ontario, Oregon. He regularly speaks to the county historical society, has been president of the county bar association, has made five country and gospel CDs, and has won numerous awards. Everywhere he goes people encourage him, and in turn he encourages everyone he meets.

"I'm a blessed man," Bill says. "My blindness taught me about new ways of seeing. . . . I've learned patience and that strength comes from struggle. I learned I could languish or I could live. . . . Life is about the choices you make hourly. You can be bitter and turn inward or turn outward. I choose to embrace life."

Bill Van Atta discovered what Viktor Frankl discovered, along with almost every other successful person: You've got to cling to positives. As Eleanor Roosevelt said, "It's better to light a candle than curse the darkness." I know far too many people who curse the darkness, so as for me, I will light a candle. And I will start today.

STEP ⓬
DRAW CLOSE TO GOD

The boy was barely alive.

Dr. Winters was called at 1:00 AM and told to rush to the hospital. His hands were the only ones in the city skilled enough to save the boy. Since every minute was crucial, he took a shortcut through one of the most dangerous neighborhoods of the city. At a stoplight a man in a dirty flannel shirt forced open the door, pulled him out of his seat, and ordered, "Give me your car!"

The doctor explained that he was on the way to the hospital for emergency surgery, but the thief wouldn't listen. He took the car and sped off. Dr. Winters ran through the streets trying to make it to the hospital on foot. An hour later he finally made it.

"You're too late," the head nurse said. "The boy died about thirty minutes ago. His father is in the chapel. He can't understand why you never came."

Dr. Winters walked to the chapel and there, weeping at the altar, was a man in a dirty flannel shirt. The boy's father looked up at the doctor and in horror realized what he had just done. He had pushed away the only one in the city who could have saved his son.

How often do we do this to God? We push him away for many reasons. Maybe we don't have time for him, we have blamed him for some misfortune, or we just don't think about him. My dear friend Pastor Ron Mehl says that we push God away by forgetting who he really is. In his book *Just in Case I Can't Be There*, he writes the following:

- I've forgotten His power . . . that He can do anything.

- I've forgotten His purpose . . . that He's up to something in my life.

- I've forgotten His presence . . . that He's always near and wants to help.

- I've forgotten His sovereignty . . . that He's always in control even when I'm not.

- I've forgotten His peace . . . that exceeds my understanding.

Pushing God away, however we do it, is self-defeating. For the core of faith is drawing close to God. The closer we get, the clearer we see and the calmer we feel. Faith gives us confidence and strength and courage. William Shakespeare wrote in his play *Henry VI* that "God shall be my hope, my stay, my guide, and lantern to my feet."

A life without God is severely limited. In fact, life doesn't make sense without God. He gives us a purpose, and without a purpose we are like a ship lost on the ocean with neither a map nor a rudder. As the actress Kathy Ireland says, "My faith is important. I have nothing without it." As I help people deal with the hurts and difficulties of life, I see even those who have no experience with him reaching up to God. When we are alone or heartbroken or overwhelmed, we yearn for closeness and comfort from the Maker of all.

James gives us the simple solution to this deep yearning: "Come close to God, and God will come close to you."[1] The Bible speaks of many ways to draw close and connect with God. Here are six important ones:

SEEK GOD

God is not hiding. David tells his son Solomon, "If you seek him, you will find him."[2] God is right next to each of us. He guides our way and guards our back. He is above us and below us. He is everywhere at every moment. I frequently ask my eleven-year-old son, "Where is God today?" Dusty gives me that what-a-stupid-question look and says, "He is in his heaven and in my heart." God is also in a beautiful sunset and the smile of a stranger. God is so big and yet so personal. Unfortunately we frequently don't see because we don't look. Yet Jeremiah writes that God is crying out, "If you look for me wholeheartedly, you will find me."[3]

Every day I wish to seek God. Wherever I am and whatever I am doing I want to find a glimpse of him. Because that glimpse, no matter how big or small, is what gives me everything I need to be whole and healthy. As David writes as he wanders in the wilderness of Judah, "Oh God . . . I earnestly search for you. My soul thirsts for you; my whole body longs for you in this parched and weary land."[4] Augustine in his *Confessions* writes, "Thou has formed us for thyself, and our hearts are restless till they find rest in thee." So much of what we seek—success, possessions, status, acceptance, respect—is ultimately empty and unfulfilling without God.

As we seek God, he seeks us. He pursues us more persistently than we pursue him. Yet God is a gentleman; he will not force himself upon us or push himself into our lives without a proper invitation. In a delightful little book, *The Air I Breathe*, Louie Giglio puts it this way: "God is always seeking you. Every sunset. Every clear blue sky. Each ocean wave. The starry host of night. He blankets each new day with the invitation, 'I am here.'" All we need to do is look and listen, for he is there.

KNOW HIM

To know a little about God is to understand a lot about everything else. As we seek God, the desire to know him deeper and deeper will consume us. Yet A. W. Tozer writes in *The Pursuit of God* that "the world is perishing for lack of the knowledge of God." J. I. Packer takes this thought a bit deeper in *Knowing God* by writing, "Disregard the study of God, and you sentence yourself to stumble and blunder through life blindfolded, as it were, with no sense of direction and no understanding of what surrounds you. This way you can waste your life and lose your soul." We must know God to know ourselves and how to live abundantly in this broken world.

In ecstasy Jim Elliot cried out in his journal, "Oh, the fullness, pleasure, sheer excitement of knowing God on earth." Knowing God involves building a relationship with him and then doing all those little things to maintain that relationship. To know God is not an academic assignment, it is something personal and emotional. It involves every aspect of who we are—our mind, heart, body, relationships, and spirit. It takes these pieces and enlarges them, filling them with meaning and purpose. Peter V. Deison wrote, "God wants us to know him deeply because he knows what knowing him will do for us."

The more we set aside time to know God, the closer we move to him.

And the closer we move the more we come to know. Yet a finite mind can never fully grasp an infinite God. We cannot conceive how great he is or how majestic his nature. Our thoughts cannot capture his power, and our words cannot express his awesomeness. We use words like infinite, holy, perfect, eternal, all-knowing, and all-powerful, but our understanding of such is so small. I do not write this to discourage but rather to keep perspective. All who are wise will strive to know God, yet they must keep in mind that this is a humbling and exhilarating task. J. I. Packer challenges us: "What makes life worthwhile is having a big enough objective, something which catches our imagination and lays hold of our allegiance; and this the Christian has in a way that no other person has. For what higher, more exalted, and compelling goal can there be than to know God?"

FEAR HIM

If we truly see God, we fear him—not because he is bad, but because he is so powerful. He holds the power of life and death. He is the judge of good and evil. After Jacob had his famous dream of an angelic staircase, he woke up and said, "'Surely the Lord is in this place, and I wasn't even aware of it!' But he was also afraid and said, 'What an awesome place this is!'"[5] We rarely grasp how incredible God is. He is so great and we are so small.

Fear is sometimes the most honest and sensible response to greatness. Solomon writes, "Fear of the Lord is the foundation of true knowledge"[6] and "Fear of the Lord is a life-giving fountain."[7] Fear can trigger awe and respect and obedience. These are healthy responses to God's character and attributes.

In his classic book *The Lion, the Witch and the Wardrobe*, C. S. Lewis includes the following conversation between Mrs. Beaver and Lucy:

"If there's anyone who can appear before Aslan without their knees knocking, they're either braver than most or else just silly."

"Then he isn't safe?" said Lucy.

"Safe? . . . Who said anything about safe? 'Course he isn't safe. But he's good."

Mark Buchanan drives the point of this fictional conversation home with the title of his book: *Your God Is Too Safe*. In his journal entitled *Devotions*, John Donne concludes that you either fear God or you fear everything else. Fear is the most sane and realistic response to an infinite, omnipotent, and eternal God.

LOVE HIM

When Jesus was asked what was the greatest of all commandments, he said that it was to "love the Lord your God with all your heart, all your soul, all your mind, and all your strength."[8] To know God is to love him with all of who we are. When we realize that in the midst of his infinite power there is gentleness and mercy, our hearts soften. God's love for us causes us to love him. What other response could one have to such an amazing love?

Out of our love comes a desire to express our delight. J. Oswald Sanders wrote, "Worship flows from love. . . . Where love is deep, worship will overflow." Love without expression becomes suspect. If love is kept quiet, it fades and may even die. The psalmist starts his worship with, "Shout with joy to the Lord" and encourages us to "come before him, "singing with joy."[9] Worship is an integral part of our faith. Amy Carmichael reminds us that without worship "we so often run dry. We do not give time enough to what makes for depth, and so we are shallow; a wind, quite a little wind, can ruffle our surface; a little hot sun, and all the moisture in us evaporates. It should not be so." Love expressed is both refreshing and delightful.

To worship God is to acknowledge him. It is to recognize his greatness and majesty and mercy in the world around us. It is to thank him for who he is and what he's done and what he will do. It is to tell others about the magnificent God of the universe.

TRUST HIM

Trust in people, and they'll let you down. Trust in things, and they'll fall apart. Trust in yourself, and you are doomed to disappointment. So what and whom can you rely on? God alone is worthy of trust. Solomon tells us to "trust in the Lord with all your heart; do not depend on your own understanding."[10] The more we get to know God, the more trustworthy we find him to be. Linda Dillow wrote, "Trusting God is a moment-by-moment challenge possible only when we focus on his character." We can trust him totally because

- he is good;

- he is in control;

- he is wise;

- he loves us;

- he is with us.

David tells us that God says, "I will guide you along the best pathway for your life. I will advise you and watch over you."[11]

To trust God is one of the smartest things you can do. Throughout Psalms God is seen as a rock, a refuge, a hiding place, a fortress, a protector, and a shelter in times of storm. He is trustworthy in the darkness, when anxieties overwhelm us, when dreams fall apart, and when nothing is going our way. God is also trustworthy during the day, when all is smooth, or when distractions pull us away. John Calvin reassures us that "trusting God allows for gratitude in prosperity, patience in adversity, and a wonderful security." As we trust God we lean on him, or as Amy Carmichael, the missionary to India, suggested: We can tuck ourselves into God. So do what François de Fénelon, the seventeenth-century French archbishop, suggested: "Pray for strength and faith enough to trust yourself completely to God. . . . Give yourself as completely as you can to God. Do so until your final breath, and he will never desert you."

FOLLOW HIM

If you truly trust God, why not follow him? As Elijah spoke to the people at Mount Carmel, he put it simply: "If the Lord is God, follow him."[12] Jesus asked people to follow him; on one occasion he said, "Take up your cross and follow me."[13] Following God means to *obey* him, *honor* him, and *imitate* him. Anyone serious about drawing closer to God will do all three of these. Each of them becomes a symbol that God is important to you.

Obey: Jesus said that "if you love me, obey my commandments"[14] and one of his greatest commandments was to "love your neighbor as yourself."[15] Therefore, I want to treat others respectfully and with kindness. I try to treat others as Jesus would treat them: with patience, understanding, encouragement, and love.

Obedience can also mean to step out of our comfort zone and take a risk to follow him. Abraham is a great example of obedience; James wrote that "he was trusting God so much that he was willing to do whatever God told him to do."[16] Remember these wise words by Michael Molinos: "Obedience is ready at any time, with no excuse and no delay."

Honor: Solomon tells us to "honor the Lord with your wealth."[17] Part of loving and following God is giving regularly to him. As we give him our time, talents, and treasures, we draw closer to him. Dag Hammarskjöld wrote in *Markings*:

> Thou takest the pen—and the lines dance,
> Thou takest the flute—and the notes shimmer,
> Thou takest the brush—and the colors sing . . .
> How then can I hold anything back from Thee.

However, honor is more than giving. Respecting God, speaking of him reverently, being aware of him, and teaching our children about his importance are all powerful ways of showing honor.

Imitate: As we follow God, we try to be like him. The psalmist wrote, "Walk only in his paths."[18] Benjamin Franklin said to "imitate Jesus." The term *Christian* refers to one being like Christ. He is our example. In the book *In His Steps*, Charles Sheldon challenges us all to ask that simple yet profound question, "What would Jesus do?"

To have a great life we must follow the words and principles of God. He is our maker, who knows us better than we know ourselves. So follow his example and listen to his words. Jesus said, "My sheep listen to my voice; I know them, and they follow me."[19] So as we struggle day by day, in whatever our circumstances, we must draw close to God. Follow him and let him be our guide.

Drawing close to God allows us to draw close to all that is good. It enriches our every experience and brings meaning to everything—regardless of how adverse or obscure. As we intentionally *seek* him, we come to know a few precious and powerful glimpses of what is ultimately beyond our limited comprehension. The more we get to know him, the more we come to fear and love and trust him. The only rational response is to follow him. Altogether these six verbs draw us closer to God and deepen our connection with the infinite. In so doing, we become attuned to his eternal voice with its wisdom and guidance and comfort. This alone makes life worthwhile.

Once Billy Graham was asked, "Of all the presidents and people you've met, of all the crusades and conferences you've held, of all the honors you've received, what was the highlight of your long and successful life?"

Without hesitation, his response was that it was his time alone during the day when he could truly draw closer to God. Everything else paled when compared to spending time connecting with the Lord and maker of the universe.

This reminds me of the words of another great minister, Charles Spurgeon. He once said that time alone in quietude "is as a palace of cedar to the wise, for along its hallowed courts the king in his beauty deigns to walk." Therefore, every day I want to walk with him and draw close to him. To have a fulfilled and abundant life, we must connect with the ultimate source of all fulfillment and abundance.

Right now, before you do anything else, reach out to God and draw close to him.

STEP **⓭**

BUILD INTEGRITY

He was known as "Honest Abe."

Abraham Lincoln had integrity. But in 1836 as he was campaigning for election to the Illinois legislature, his opponent claimed to have evidence of Lincoln's dishonesty. This opponent then promised to keep it confidential as a favor. Yet Lincoln wrote him a letter insisting that any personal failure that might cause people to question his character should be immediately disclosed. Lincoln didn't fear exposure because he had integrity. Lincoln had challenged his opponent, who quickly admitted he was bluffing.

Various studies have shown that people value integrity in a leader more than anything else. Integrity is the core of character and the glue that ultimately holds together all healthy relationships. We listen to, trust, and are drawn to those with integrity. We like them and respect them. I was recently at a banquet celebrating marriage where one of the speakers explained what he loved most about his wife. After he shared a list of wonderful things he said, "Let me sum it up—integrity is her middle name." What a great compliment.

God loves integrity. Solomon writes that God hates things that oppose integrity, such as "a lying tongue, . . . a heart that plots evil, feet that race to do wrong, a false witness who pours out lies."[1]

Integrity starts internally, but it is ultimately determined by how we live—our decisions, our words, and our actions. Dan Gater wrote, "Integrity is what we do, what we say, and what we say we do." The word *integrity* comes from a root that means whole, complete, and mature. When a person has integrity, he is solid, trustworthy, and has a low probability of disappointing others. Solomon wrote in another place that "people with integrity walk safely, but those who follow crooked paths will slip and fall."[2] Integrity is a solid rock on which you can anchor every aspect of your life as well as a compass, which can provide you direction and keep you from getting lost.

Lack of integrity is dangerous. Sooner or later it will destroy your character, your relationships, and your dreams. Integrity must be holistic. Partial integrity is really a lack of integrity, and it's like a rotten spot on an apple; it must be cut out, or it will soon spoil the whole apple. We must try to build integrity into every aspect of our life. We must ask ourselves if we demonstrate integrity in

- work
- marriage
- finances
- sexuality
- recreation
- adversity
- faith
- parenthood
- friendship
- communication
- conflict
- tough decisions
- the details of life

Integrity in every aspect of your day is central to a great life. It gives you joy while it earns the love and respect of others. Integrity makes you decide what kind of person you want to be. Integrity is sometimes costly in terms of money, relationships, or position, but ultimately a life of integrity leads to more abundance than anything you may have lost in the process. There are many aspects of integrity, but here are four that will help you build this virtue:

SHOW HONESTY

During the depression a department store in Philadelphia decided to have a large sale. Some of the items it wished to advertise were dollar neckties reduced to a quarter. This store had a reputation for integrity, so the man who was writing the advertising for this sale decided to check out the merchandise.

"Are these ties any good?" the man asked the buyer.

"No, they're not," came back the buyer's honest reply.

The ad man could not write anything he knew was false, so this is what he composed: "They are not as good as they look, but they are good enough at 25 cents."

The sale was a huge success, and the ties were in such great demand that they sold out quickly with hundreds of customers placing additional orders for the famous cheap ties. The store learned that honesty works.

I don't need to convince anybody of the value of honesty. We all know the importance of truth and the dangers of dishonesty. The core of the ninth commandment is "Don't lie." Your parents taught you this; so did your teachers and friends and everybody else. Then why do we lie? Here are a few reasons:

- To look better than we are

- To avoid trouble or disappointment

- To protect someone or something

- To get something we want

- To feel better about ourselves

Lies only work for a short time: Ultimately dishonesty is always exposed. Baltasar Gracian, a seventeenth-century Spanish philosopher, wrote: "A single lie destroys a reputation of integrity." If you are a person of integrity, you will show honesty regardless of your circumstances, your pressures, your needs, or others' expectations. The book of Proverbs says that "honesty guides good people."[3]

This morning while I was at a local grocery store a woman approached the cashier and said, "I was here a few minutes ago, and I didn't get charged for one of my items."

"Thank you for being so honest," the cashier said. "But why did you come back?"

"I have found that honesty pays," she said, smiling. "If I'm honest with people, they'll be honest with me."

Honesty not only pays, but it's the right thing to do. Dishonesty can spread in more ways than blatant lying. It can spread through

- silence

- passivity

- exaggeration

- gossip

- misunderstanding

- assumption

H. Jackson Brown Jr. encourages us to "live so that when your children think of fairness and honesty, they think of you."

ACT AUTHENTICALLY

I recently attended a national convention and met with a group of respected leaders for lunch at a small restaurant. At another table sat a man who has a history of ignoring me. During lunch he approached my table and greeted me in a warm, positive way. I was shocked but delighted. I introduced him to my friends and thought that perhaps I had misjudged this man.

However, during the next week, I ran into this man three times and greeted him by name. Each time he ignored me and wouldn't even acknowledge me. You see, he wasn't interested in me because I don't have a lot of power or influence. But my friends did. By greeting me, he knew I would introduce him to those at my table. His lack of authenticity angers me. He is warm to me when I'm with others, yet ignores me when I'm alone. We call that two-faced or hypocritical.

When someone acts differently in public than in private, he lacks integrity. In fact, according to the field of psychology, the greater the gap between a person's public and private self, the greater his or her emotional immaturity or lack of trustworthiness. Character is who you are when no one is looking. Ron Mehl writes in *Just in Case I Can't Be There*: "The most significant choices you make in life won't be made in the middle of a crowd, with lots of people standing around. They will be made in the private times when only God sees what you are doing." Therefore live in such a way that there are no secrets and that all you say or do in private could be told in public without embarrassment.

LIVE MORALLY AND ETHICALLY

In 1775 there was a heated campaign for the Virginia assembly. In the midst of a debate a forty-three-year-old colonel named George Washington said something that offended an older gentleman, William Payne. This man exploded, attacking Washington with a hickory stick and knocking him to the ground. Washington had to hold back his lieutenants, who wished to avenge the honor of their leader. But Washington assured them that he would take care of the situation.

The next day Washington wrote a letter asking Mr. Payne to meet at a local tavern. The older gentleman agreed to this meeting, expecting that an apology would be demanded and he would be challenged to a duel. He was shocked when Washington apologized for offending him. The future president said, "Mr. Payne, to err is natural; to rectify error is glory." Then Washington reached out his hand and indicated that he hoped he would be forgiven. William Payne shook Washington's hand, and the two soon became great friends. George Washington did what was good and right.

The heart of integrity is to do good. David tells us to "turn away from evil and do good."[4] Yet this is not profound news. Isn't this what your parents told you since you were a small child? It's a simple concept but difficult to put into practice. Paul encourages us to "hate what is wrong. Hold tightly to what is good."[5] John Wesley preached that we should do all the good we can, by all the means we can, in every place we can, at all the times we can, to everyone we can, as long as we ever can.

As we resist evil and choose good, we demonstrate integrity. To do good when it is hard is the best test of integrity. Sometimes we don't feel like doing good, or we can't find any good to do. But with God's help we will act with integrity. Tryon Edwards says, "Between two evils, do neither." The prophet Amos writes, "Do what is good and run from evil."[6]

The flip side of doing good is doing right. Good has to do with the heart, and right has to do with the mind. In the best of all situations, they are the same. It is important to do good, but goodness, unless anchored to something solid, can appear to shift. What feels or looks good one day might not feel or look good the next. What is right should always be right, for it is based on universal principles and God's eternal truth. Therefore, do all you can to anchor goodness to what is right.

The importance of truth is echoed in the words of many who are wise. George Eliot wrote: "Keep true, never be ashamed of doing right." Yet there is often great pressure to acquiesce to popular opinion or others' expectations. William J. H. Boetcker advised: "It is better to displease the people by doing what you know is right, than to temporarily please them by doing what you know is wrong." Thomas Jefferson wrote, "In matters of principle, stand like a rock; in matters of taste, swim with the current." But standing like a rock is hard, and we have all been tempted to choose the easier wrong over the harder right. Theodore Hesburgh says it most eloquently with these words: "My basic principle is that you don't make decisions because they are easy; you don't make them because they are cheap; you don't make them because they are popular; you make them because they're right." Ultimately, there is never a truly good reason for not doing right.

TAKE RESPONSIBILITY

Richard Nixon did some great things as president of the United States, but his administration will forever be seen in the light of Watergate. During the 1972 presidential campaign, Nixon approved a break-in of the Democratic headquarters at the Watergate Hotel in Washington DC. This second-rate burglary soon exploded into a national crisis. How did this happen?

It all came down to integrity. As the investigation ensued, recorded conversations between Nixon and his closest advisors were made public. People were shocked at the president's obscenities, cover-ups, and unethical responses. If Nixon had been honest and admitted his role in the Watergate crimes, he might have saved his presidency. Ultimately it was his lack of integrity that forced him to resign. When we fail, we have a tendency to hide or blame. Some avoid people and try to cover up their failures, often making them worse in the process. Others look for anyone or anything they might blame—parents, a spouse, the children, the government, society, the weather, God. Hiding and blaming are immature responses. We all fail. We all fall. Each of us has been dishonest or hypocritical and done what was evil or wrong. An immature response is to hide and run. A mature response is to face our failures and take responsibility for them. Another U.S. president, Harry Truman, had a plaque on his desk that read "The buck stops here." In other words, "I'll take responsibility." That attitude requires courage and integrity. Yet it is through admitting our failures that we can

- heal wounds;

- right wrongs;

- seek forgiveness;

- change behaviors;

- learn lessons;

- strengthen character;

- encourage growth;

- draw closer to God.

Taking responsibility for a situation, even if our part was only a small piece, allows us to begin to regain our integrity.

In the novel *The Wedding* by Nicholas Sparks, the lead character discovers that his wife has fallen out of love with him. Yet he is determined to take responsibility and win her back. In a key conversation toward the end of the book, he says, "I haven't been the best husband, and . . . I guess I'm trying to change."

"Why?" she asked. . . .

"Because," [he] said after a moment, "you and the kids are the most important people in the world to me—you always have been—and I've wasted too many years acting as if you weren't. I know I can't change the past, but I can change the future. I can change, too. And I will."

This man's willingness to take responsibility and change his behavior showed his integrity and ended up saving his marriage. We cannot erase our past failures, but we can face them, admit them, and establish a life of integrity from this point forward.

In the book of Genesis we learn about Joseph, a young man committed to integrity no matter what the cost. His older brothers became jealous of him and sold him to slave traders, who in turn sold him to the captain of the palace guard in Egypt. Yet Joseph showed such great integrity and responsibility that the captain placed him in charge of his entire household, all his business dealings, and everything he owned. Not long after this, the captain's wife began trying to seduce him, but Joseph refused to respond. One day she became more aggressive, and when he resisted, she was so furious at his rejection that she had him imprisoned. Even in jail, Joseph showed such responsibility that he was soon placed in a leadership position.

Several years later he was able to get an audience with the king, and by the time the audience was over, he was given the second highest position in all of Egypt. His wisdom and foresight saved the country from famine. Later, when he welcomed the brothers who had betrayed him, he didn't act vindictively toward them. When his father was on his deathbed, he blessed Joseph by calling him "a prince among his brothers." He also said that though "Archers attacked him savagely . . . his bow remained taut."[7]

Joseph courageously and consistently lived his integrity. This was not always easy or comfortable. Yet he did it—with his words or actions, in public and private, whether popular or not. Integrity is an intentional choice to follow a healthy path. A person with integrity has hope. Anne Lamott wrote, "Hope begins in the dark, the stubborn hope that if you just show up and try to do the right thing, the dawn will come. You wait and watch and work. You don't give up." That last sentence is crucial, for if you have integrity, you will be less likely to give up. A person with this type of character tries to do the good and right thing regardless of the situation. None of us can ever do this perfectly; but the longer we practice integrity, the more naturally it integrates into our life. This is a moment-by-moment struggle all the days of our life. The last words of Grover Cleveland probably reflect the thoughts of many of us: "I have tried so hard to do the right."

STEP ⑭

CULTIVATE COMMUNITY

Bill and Jim were buddies.

They both fought in the trenches of World War I. One day as they charged the enemy, the firefight was severe. The commanding officer called for his men to retreat to their trenches. As they followed their orders, Jim was shot. He fell to the ground, unable to get himself to a place of safety. Bill made it back to the trenches and was shocked to discover that his good friend hadn't.

The shelling continued. The battle grew worse. Bill could see Jim lying unprotected, all alone in the middle of a horrible battlefield. Bill wanted to go out and help him, comfort him, encourage him. The commanding officer refused to let Bill leave the trenches. He said, "It's too dangerous, and besides, Jim is dying. It's too late for him. You're a good soldier, and I won't lose you trying to save someone who has been fatally wounded."

Ignoring his orders, Bill faced the bullets and ran for his friend. With great risk and courage Bill dragged Jim back to the safety of the trenches, but it was too late. Jim was dead. The officer was furious. "What were you thinking? What a stupid risk! Now don't you see what a worthless chance you took?" Bill responded firmly, "It was definitely worth the risk."

"Are you crazy?" asked the commanding officer.

"No," Bill insisted. "It was worth the risk because Jim's last words were, 'Thank you; I knew you'd come.'"

If you're part of a community, you know someone will come. You will not be alone but will always have a place to belong. We were all designed to connect with others. Connection is life and isolation is death. It is in community that we experience the greatest growth and joy. M. Scott Peck writes in his book *The Different Drum* that "we humans hunger for genuine community and will work hard to maintain it precisely because it is the way to live most fully, most vibrantly."

We all yearn for intimate allies and deep friendships with those willing to share their lives. We hope for companions to journey alongside us as we scale the rugged peaks and trek the empty deserts of life. We long for a band of brothers to protect our back and fight beside us. This is what John Eldredge calls "fellowships of the heart," and it's what we passionately crave and desperately dream. In Connecting, Larry Crabb writes, "The greatest need in modern civilization is the development of communities—true communities where the heart of God is home, where the humble and wise learn to shepherd those on the path behind them, where trusting strugglers lock arms with others as together they journey on." After all, we need a place

- to be loved when we're lonely;
- to be protected when we're afraid;
- to be comforted when we're hurting;
- to be taught when we're confused;
- to be encouraged when we're downhearted;
- to be given hope when all seems dark.

True community can provide all of this. Yet community doesn't just happen; it must be carefully and intentionally cultivated. In his book *Waking the Dead*, John Eldredge writes, "A true community is something you'll have to fight for. You'll have to fight to get one, and you'll have to fight to keep it afloat." But it's noble, life-affirming, and truly worth fighting for. How do we develop a community? Through sharing, forgiving, offering comfort, and challenging each other.

SHARING OUR HEARTS

Healthy communication is crucial to building positive relationships. Without it there is no hope for cultivating community. It's through our words that we get to know, understand, and encourage each other. We share our hearts with each other and go beyond the trap of sharing only facts, incidents, gossip, or trivia. This sort of small talk has its place, but after a while it is not truly satisfying. It gives the illusion of connection, but it does not provide closeness. I yearn for something more. I want to know your opinions and how you got them. I wish to understand who and what has influenced you most throughout your life. I hope to hear about your worries and fears, your strengths and weakness, your passions and dreams. I simply desire to know what makes you tick. Then I can love and accept the real you, not a fuzzy vapor that disappears when my arms stretch out for a genuine embrace.

It's easy for me to embrace others, but I'm afraid to let you embrace me. I don't know if I can trust you. Too many people have betrayed me in the past, so why should I trust that you won't do the same? When I want to connect, all sorts of emotions get in the way—mistrust, hurt, fear, defensiveness, insecurity, jealousy, guilt, shame, disappointment, frustration. As John Powell writes in *Why I Am Afraid to Tell You Who I Am*, "If I tell you who I am, you may not like who I am, and it's all I have." Fifty-seven pages later he writes that "to reveal myself openly and honestly takes the rawest kind of courage."

To cultivate community, I must admit who I am to myself and then confess it to others. I must stop hiding and risk total humiliation. I must step out in faith and expose my dark side, as Brennan Manning does in his book *Ruthless Trust: The Ragamuffin's Path to God*, when he cries out, "Is there anyone I can level with? Anyone I dare tell that I am benevolent and malevolent, chaste and randy, compassionate and vindictive, selfless and selfish, that beneath my brave words lives a frightened child, that I dabble in religion and pornography, that I have blackened a friend's character, betrayed a trust, violated a confidence, that I am tolerant and thoughtful, a bigot and a blowhard. . . ?"

People can be so cruel and judgmental. I've heard them stab each other in the back, betray confidences, belittle friends, reject those they disagree with, and emotionally beat up those whom they don't understand. I love people; I just don't trust them. So what can I do? In the end I have to take a risk because I know M. Scott Peck is right when he says that "community requires the ability to expose our wounds and weaknesses to our fellow creatures."

Communities must be places of safety. This is where we accept each other as we are with no conditions. This is where we say, "Come as you are. I will stand beside you, and nothing you can do will push me away from you." In his book *Sacred Companions*, David G. Benner says that we all need "a place where anything can be said without fear of criticism or ridicule. It is a place where it is safe to share deepest secrets, darkest fears, most acute sources of shame, most disturbing questions or anxieties. It is a place of grace—a place where others are accepted as they are for the sake of who they may become."

I want a place like this. Every Saturday morning at 6:00 AM. I meet with eight other guys, and we try to create a place like this. It is hard, and we struggle. We haven't figured out how to do it all the time, but every once in a while we discover community, and when we do, it is wonderful. John Winthrop, the first governor of the Massachusetts Bay Colony, gave these words to his fellow colonists in 1630: "We must delight in each other, make others' conditions our own, rejoice together, mourn together, labor and suffer together, always having before our eyes . . . our community." In a perfect world, community would be the norm rather than the exception. It all must start with sharing our time and our hearts with each other, our family, our friends, our coworkers, our neighbors, and our church. So open up and connect as you

- pray together

- play together

- walk together

- serve together

- struggle together

- cry together

- talk together

- dream together

FORGIVING EACH OTHER

Life is full of hurts. Every day, in a hundred random and thoughtless ways, people inflict pain on each other. Holding on to this pain distances us from others. To cultivate community and build trust, we must forgive.

It may sound strange, but the first step toward forgiving is to admit how hurt and angry we really are. The fact is, others have been insensitive and cruel. Sometimes it seems easier to pretend the hurt isn't important and try to forget about it. The trouble is, we don't forget. Offenses that wound our heart accumulate in our memory and keep us from experiencing community. Forgiveness essentially means giving up our right to make other people pay for the wrongs they have committed against us. It's a choice, a decision of the will. Keep in mind that the choice of forgiveness almost always precedes the feeling of forgiveness. That may take time—not because forgiveness doesn't work, but because your emotional wounds still need time to heal.

We must stop rehearsing the pain. Once we have faced what has happened to us, we can be done with reliving the past and rehashing the details. Memories will rise in our mind, but we can choose to put them away and focus on other things. We can then, slowly and cautiously, start the journey toward community.

Sometimes we don't want to forgive. Forgiveness may be difficult for us because

- we are afraid of being hurt again;

- we're still angry;

- we don't want to admit our hurt;

- we think the other person doesn't deserve forgiveness;

- the offender's apology doesn't seem sincere;

- certain things seem too big to forgive.

In spite of our struggles to forgive, the apostle Paul tells us, "Be kind to each other, tenderhearted, forgiving one another, just as God through Christ has forgiven you."[1] Besides, if we refuse to forgive others, why should God be willing to forgive us? Forgiveness sets both the offender and the victim free. When we forgive, something inside of us changes.

We are set free from the bile and bitterness that eats away at us. We are liberated from the obsession, sleeplessness, and frustration that can so easily consume us. When we forgive, we are able to see others more clearly. Forgiveness allows us to step out and grow. If you hold something against someone, you will find it hard to trust them. You will constantly guard yourself from the next potential hurt. This is why Martin Luther King Jr. said, "Forgiveness is not an occasional act; it is a permanent attitude."

Forgiveness works both ways. Just as we need to forgive, there are times we need to seek forgiveness. When we become aware that we have hurt someone, even if it was not intentional, we need to do what we can to heal the situation. The "Five Rs" allow anyone who has hurt another to take a giant step toward restoration:

1. **Responsibility:** Accept that your actions or attitudes did harm, regardless of whether the injured person deserved it or had a part in it.
2. **Repentance:** Sincerely and specifically apologize to the person you harmed without blame, excuses, or defensiveness.
3. **Remorse:** Try to see the situation through the injured person's eyes and feel the hurt that he or she feels.
4. **Restitution:** Do something special and meaningful for the person harmed to show that you genuinely regret what you did.
5. **Repair:** Do all you can to return the relationship to the state it was in before the injury.

Lack of forgiveness, either giving it or asking for it, builds walls and blocks community. On the other hand, forgiveness breaks down those walls, allowing compassion, connection, and community to happen.

COMFORTING EACH OTHER

In true community, you feel loved and accepted. You belong. If you are hurting or struggling, others will quickly come alongside you. In community, loneliness is lessened and sometimes even taken away. When a person sees a need, he or she quickly and sacrificially meets it. In a community, people come alongside others without having to be asked. Paul writes about this sort of love and acceptance in 1 Thessalonians: "Brothers and sisters, we urge you to warn those who are lazy. Encourage those who are timid. Take tender care of those who are weak. Be patient with everyone."[2]

Community involves binding together with love and loyalty. We commit time, communication, and comfort to each other. The New Testament reaffirms the importance of comfort when it says, "So encourage each other" and "[God] comforts us in all our troubles so that we can comfort others."[3] Comfort is love in action. It asks, "What are you doing for others?" It makes love real—not sentimental or romantic but sacrificial and hardworking. A community without love ceases to be a community. Dr. Willard Harley writes in his book *Love Busters* that there are six things that can kill the love in any relationship or community:

① Selfish demands
② Disrespectful judgments
③ Angry outbursts
④ Dishonesty
⑤ Annoying habits
⑥ Independent behavior

Love defers to others, and their needs take precedence over yours. In a community there is an interdependence of love.

Comfort and friendship each grow out of the other. Friendship is like shade on a hot day. Solomon says that "a friend is always loyal."[4] A friend knows what we need and doesn't hesitate to provide it. In his book *Our Greatest Gift*, Henri Nouwen writes about such a friend: "During the most difficult period of my life, when I experienced great anguish and despair, he was there. Many times, he pulled my head to his chest and prayed for me without words but with a Spirit-filled silence that dispelled my demons of despair and made me rise up from his embrace with new vitality." This is the sort of friendship and comfort we all yearn for. This is what community is all about. I love the words of Albert Schweitzer: "Sometimes our light goes out but is blown into flame by another human being." The joy of community is that it will not allow your light to be out for very long.

CHALLENGING EACH OTHER

Members of a healthy community challenge each other to a stronger and better life. They want the best for others and therefore speak the truth in love. They gently and compassionately warn of potential peril, point out blind spots, share different perspectives, and ask the hard questions. Stu Webber says that "friends are divinely placed guardrails"—they keep us from going off a cliff. Sometimes the most loving thing a friend can do is confront. David Benner writes, "Love cannot ignore things that are self-destructive in the loved one." Perhaps this is what Solomon meant when he wrote, "Wounds from a friend can be trusted."[5]

I just returned from my Saturday morning men's group, and it was hard. Several of the guys were confronted with loving brutality about their negative attitude toward women. The confronters were direct and firm and respectful, stating what they observed and why they thought it was wrong. One of the guys squirmed and tried to justify his attitude, but nobody would let him off the hook. We love this guy, but this morning we caused discomfort. Solomon says that "as iron sharpens iron, so a friend sharpens a friend."[6] Through the sharpening process comes friction and sparks—things get hot. Yet confrontation is not done to belittle, humiliate, or discourage.

A community remains calm and close when weakness is visible. It believes that strength lies just below the surface. It uses challenge to help others become all that God wants them to be. R. C. H. Lenski wrote, "It is the best and truest friend who honestly tells us the truth about ourselves even when he knows we shall not like it. False friends are the ones who hide such truth from us and do so in order to remain in our favor."

There must be days when you are the challenger and days when you are the one being challenged. Many refer to this as "accountability." In *Living Above the Level of Mediocrity*, Chuck Swindoll writes about the four qualities necessary for accountability:

1. **Vulnerability:** capable of being wounded, shown to be wrong, even admitting it before being confronted
2. **Teachability:** a willingness to learn, being quick to hear and respond to reproof, being open to counsel

③ **Availability:** accessible, touchable, able to be interrupted

④ **Honesty:** committed to the truth regardless of how much it hurts, a willingness to admit the truth no matter how difficult or humiliating the admission may be

Community members use accountability to challenge each other to walk in the light. Questions provide one of the best ways to challenge each other. Ask how others have been doing during the past week in critical areas such as the following:

- anger
- pride/selfishness
- priorities
- compromises
- marriage
- health
- parenting
- anxiety/fear
- attitude
- integrity
- temptations
- finances
- addictions
- purity
- goals
- relationship with God

Challenges improve you. They make you stronger, deeper, warmer. Challenges also improve community, for the healthier the community the more it will share, forgive, and comfort.

In 1942, as Nazis occupied Holland, two families fled their homes and went into hiding in what came to be known as the "Secret Annex." For two years these families lived, isolated from the rest of the world in an old office building. Here in the shadow of discovery and death, thirteen-year-old Anne Frank wrote about her little community—how they shared their hearts and encouraged each other. Their time together was not easy, but they grew close. They learned the importance of acceptance, support, and shared optimism. In so doing, they made a horrible situation tolerable and even enjoyable.

Community can happen anywhere and at any time. If you are willing to cultivate community, ordinary times will take on a deeper meaning, and difficult times will not be without hope.

STEP ⑮

BE COMMITTED

Lieutenant Hiroo Onoda was a committed soldier. In 1944 he was stationed alone on the tropical island of Lubang in the Philippines with orders to wage guerrilla warfare against American forces. He did his job well, hiding in the jungle and making solitary raids whenever possible. In 1945 World War II ended, but LT Onoda would not give up. For twenty-nine years he followed the orders given by his commander, refusing to believe that Japan had lost the war. Living off the land and avoiding search parties, he remained committed to his cause.

Leaflets, newspapers, and letters from friends were dropped into the jungle begging LT Onoda to surrender. Yet he remained faithful to his mission. It wasn't until March 10, 1974, when he received personal orders from his former commander, that LT Onoda came out of the jungle, unloaded his bullets, and laid his gun down on the ground. His thirty-year war was finally over.

Now that's commitment!

Another man on another continent wrote the following letter to his girl-friend explaining why he must break up with her: "There is one thing in which I am in dead earnest about, and that is the communist cause. It is my life, my business, my religion, my hobby, my sweetheart, my wife, my mistress, my bread and meat. I work at it in the daytime and dream of it at night. Its hold on me grows, not lessens, as time goes on; therefore, I cannot carry on a friendship, a love affair, or even a conversation without relating it to this force which both drives and guides my life. I evaluate people, looks, ideas, and actions according to how they affect the communist cause, and by their attitude toward it. I've already been in jail because of my ideals, and if necessary, I'm ready to go before a firing squad."

Commitment or lack of commitment defines who we are. Commitments come in many different forms. LT Onoda was committed to his country, the young man to his ideology. Others may be committed to possessions, politics, hobbies, sports, jobs, health, or the most recent fad. I admire committed people. Their dedication shows that they believe in something, even if I disagree with them or think their belief is trivial. A commitment involves at least three of the following. You must

- focus your attention on it;

- not allow anyone or anything to distract you from it;

- make it your priority;

- give all of yourself to it;

- lay your money, reputation, comfort, or life down for it;

- promise to be true to it, being as dependable and trustworthy as you possibly can;

- stand up for it, regardless of what others think, say, or do;

- long to pursue it;

- let it become a part of you, as you become a part of it;

- do whatever is necessary to protect, defend, encourage, or uplift it.

We all need commitments. As Peter Marshall wrote, "A man cannot live negatively, just in terms of what he is against. The more pertinent question is, what is he for?" To have no commitments is to have no beliefs, no passions, no purposes, and ultimately, no real life. You become shallow, mediocre, and meaningless. The apostle John refers to this lack of commitment when he writes Jesus' words to one of the ancient churches: "I know all the things you do, that you are neither hot nor cold. I wish that you were one or the other! But since you are like lukewarm water, neither hot nor cold, I will spit you out of my mouth!"[1]

Though the quality of your commitment is significant, its object can make it appear either admirable or foolish. Three of the healthiest and most admirable objects of commitment are marriage, family, and God. These commitments are foundational to a wise and abundant life.

COMMIT TO MARRIAGE

A number of years ago I was at a major conference of marriage counselors where the topic was at what point a marriage should be dissolved. The speaker suggested that marriage was a contract, and when the contract was no longer beneficial to either party it should be terminated. Most of those in attendance seemed to agree. I sat in silence until I could handle it no more. I raised my hand and asked, "What about commitment?"

What happened next shocked me and has disturbed me ever since. The crowd burst into laughter. How sad!

Marriage is sacred. Jesus said, "Therefore what God has joined together, let man not separate."[2] Marriage is a total, timeless commitment between a husband and wife; it is also a covenant with God. It must be taken seriously, because God takes it seriously. T. S. Eliot wrote, "Marriage is the greatest test in the world . . . it is a test of the whole character and affects every action." A good marriage is not easy. It requires overcoming all that can potentially harm your relationship, like hectic schedules, disappointment, laziness, selfishness, negativity, boredom, debt, misunderstandings, and the gradual distancing.

In their book *When Bad Things Happen to Good Marriages*, Drs. Les and Leslie Parrott write, "A good marriage is made up of . . . two people living the love they promised. They are a committed couple." This promise involves a serious commitment to the following ten areas:

① **Oneness:** Cling to one another in body, soul, and spirit.
② **Affirmation:** Speak the truth in love, seeking to encourage each other in all you say.
③ **Togetherness:** Set aside quality time for just the two of you to enjoy romance, laughter, listening, sharing, and companionship.
④ **Prioritizing:** Put each other above everything else in your lives except for God.

⑤ **Nurturing:** Actively nurture and improve your relationship by attending seminars, studying marriage books, and discovering other resources that will strengthen your marriage.

⑥ **Faithfulness:** Do not hurt your relationship by engaging in activities that could lead to physical or emotional intimacy outside your marriage.

⑦ **Honesty:** Refuse to lie, deceive one another, or keep secrets from each other.

⑧ **Protection:** Protect each other physically, financially, emotionally, socially, and spiritually.

⑨ **Fellowship:** Get involved in a good church or group where you can find friends who value marriage and family.

⑩ **Endurance:** Take seriously your promise to love and cherish one another for all the days of your life "until death do us part."

Herman H. Kieval sums up all these areas by simply saying that "marriage is a commitment—a decision to do, all through life, that which will express love for one's spouse." In other words, you say to your spouse, "No matter what happens, I will love you."

A commitment to marriage is a promise of unconditional love and acceptance. Dan Allender and Tremper Longman III say that it "requires a radical commitment to love our spouses as they are, while longing for them to become what they are not yet." Last summer my parents celebrated their fiftieth anniversary, and we threw a great party. Like any couple, they have had their ups and downs, but through the years they have discovered that they truly do belong together. George Eliot said it beautifully with these words from *Adam Bede:* "What greater thing is there for two human souls than to feel that they are joined for life—to strengthen each other in all labor, to rest on each other in all sorrow, to minister to each other in all pain."

COMMIT TO FAMILY

Once upon a time there was a town at the foot of a mountain range that got its water from springs high in the hills. The town hired a certain forest dweller to be the Keeper of the Springs. He visited each spring, clearing the springs of fallen leaves, mud, and any other debris. Then he made sure the water flowed properly—clean, cold, and pure.

But one day the town council decided it no longer needed a Keeper of the Springs and dismissed him. Soon the water grew brown, slime filled the pipes, and an epidemic spread through the town. Recognizing a mistake had been made, the council quickly rehired the Keeper of the Springs. Within a week the water turned clear, the pipes were cleaned, and the sickness began to fade. From that point on, the town recognized the Keeper of the Springs' full value.

Each and every parent, grandparent, uncle, and aunt is a Keeper of the Springs for the children in their life. We need to proactively guard and protect our children from the dangers, foolishness, and evil that so often surround us in this broken world. We need adults who will truly commit themselves to the next generation. Dr. James Dobson writes in his book *Parenting Isn't for Cowards* that "parents can and must train, shape, mold, correct, guide, punish, reward, instruct, warn, teach, and love their kids during the formative years." Children will remember and appreciate the care we showed them more than all the stuff we give them. Adults have a powerful impact on children and teenagers. Gary Smalley and John Trent remind us that "affirming words . . . are like light switches. Speak a word of affirmation at the right moment in a child's life, and it's like lighting up a whole roomful of possibilities."

Being committed to family can be a challenge, but to ignore the challenge is to scar the future. Commitment to children requires sacrifice, discomfort, confrontation, humility, and disappointment. In the process it can produce laughter, joy, and satisfaction. Children need an atmosphere that allows them to grow strong, with branches that reach out and roots that dig deep. As you try to establish this atmosphere for your family, consider practicing the "Six As of Parenting":

① **Be Aware:** Study your children. They're wonderful creations. Listen to them, watch them, ask them questions. Talk with them, not to them. Discover their likes and dislikes, their dreams and fears, their strengths and weaknesses. Recognize how special they are.

② **Be Assertive:** Pass on the lessons you've learned from life. Teach your children the truth. Provide reasonable rules and consistent consequences when those rules are broken. Give your children security without being rigid, insensitive, abusive, angry, or exasperating.

③ **Be Accepting:** Focus on their positives and assist them with their negatives. Don't expect perfection from them lest they turn and expect it from you. Remember that children are often immature, and teenagers are frequently impulsive. Be patient with them.

④ **Be Approachable:** One of the biggest challenges dads face is maintaining too much emotional distance from their children. Be close to them. Spend quality time with them. Laugh with them; play with them; enjoy them. Take them on walks and outings and vacations. Connect with them.

⑤ **Be Affectionate:** Hug them often, and tell them you love them every day. Give them compliments, and encourage them instead of criticizing them. Don't yell, hit, name call, or belittle them. Treat them gently and with respect. Treasure them.

⑥ **Be Alert:** The world is full of dangers and temptations. Be your children's protector. Watch over them, and warn them. Protect them without being paranoid.

Most important of all, pray for them daily.

We feel differently about ourselves and our life when we know someone is praying for us. I believe one of the most powerful gifts we can give children is our committed prayers. Here are ten areas we can bring to God daily on behalf of our children, whether they are eight minutes old or eighty years old:

① their health
② their temptations
③ their safety
④ their contentment
⑤ their choices
⑥ their friends

⑦   their faith

⑧   their mate or future mate

⑨   their character

⑩   their legacy

As Solomon wrote, "Children are a gift from the Lord."[3] Therefore, commit yourself to them, and every day pray for them. Remember, they are the future.

COMMIT TO GOD

It was a Sunday morning in 1991. The small group of thirty Christians stood unafraid on the street in Cano, Peru. They wanted the world to see that they were committed. They prayed and sang to God, in spite of the fact that some twelve hours before, terrorists had killed their pastor and burned down their church and many of their houses. These people had no pastor, no more church, no more houses. Yet they continued to gather together because nobody could take away their commitment.

Every week millions of Christians gather in other countries under threat of death. Each week thousands of Christians are killed simply because they are committed to God. True commitment is being willing to pay the price. A committed Christian doesn't pray that life will be easy but rather that he or she will be strong and worthy of Christ's name. As Saleema, a nineteen-year-old Christian in Pakistan, put it, "I would rather be hung than betray my Lord." To many people throughout this world, being committed to God means suffering, persecution, beatings, imprisonment, loss of friends, destruction of possessions, and possible death. Mother Teresa defined commitment as "Jesus is everything."

There are two types of Christians: convenient Christians and committed Christians. Most of us are more convenient than committed. We give what is easy and comfortable and left over. We don't suffer much. Our faith fits effortlessly into our lives beside all our other obligations and activities. We can hardly even imagine the struggles in persecuted nations. Yet David writes, "Commit everything you do to the Lord."[4] And Paul writes, "Give your bodies to God because of all he has done for you. Let them be a living and holy sacrifice."[5] Maybe this is what Isaac Watts, the sixteenth-century hymn writer, was referring to when he wrote "Love so amazing, so divine; demands my soul, my life, my all."

So commitment is giving yourself totally to God. Oswald Chambers wrote, "Shut out every other consideration and keep yourself before God for this one thing only—My Utmost for His Highest. I am determined to be absolutely and entirely for Him and Him alone." This involves fully trusting that God is exactly who he says he is. Rick Warren writes in *The Purpose-Driven Life* that you are only committed—or surrendered—"when you rely on God to work things out instead of trying to manipulate others, force your agenda and control the situation." To be committed to God you must surrender and submit. As Jesus said, "You must turn from your selfish ways, take up your cross, and follow me."[6] We must follow his call to:

- **Adventure:** The life of faith is full of thrills and excitement. You never know exactly what to expect, for as soon as you think you have it figured out, God surprises you with something you never thought possible. To follow him is to experience life to the fullest, reaching the potential he planned for you, and never regretting a moment of it.

- **Sacrifice:** God asks us to sacrifice everything—our thoughts, emotions, body, relationships, and spirit. As we do this, he gives back to us with wisdom and generosity that makes us realize how foolish we were to question our sacrifice.

- **Servanthood:** Jesus told us that the last shall be first, the weak shall be strong, the least shall be the greatest. As we sacrifice all, we learn how to serve all. This journey of love fulfills us, giving us meaning and purpose and a peace that surpasses our comprehension.

- **Battle:** We are in the midst of a powerful, life-changing spiritual battle. Every thought and every emotion is being fought over. Each day there are victories and casualties. If we aren't prepared, we become useless. Yet if we are ready, we can wield a force that can have a remarkable impact on today and eternity.

A committed Christian must follow Christ into each of the above areas. Dallas Willard wrote, "The secret . . . is to learn from Christ how to live our total lives, how to invest all our time and energies of mind and body as he did." That's commitment.

Rachel Scott decided to give it all to God. She wrote in her journal that she wanted a true commitment that went beyond just nice words and good intentions. She was hurt when friends rejected her because of this, but she wrote, "I will take it."

On April 20, 1999, another student approached Rachel at Columbine High School. He held a gun to her head and asked her if she still believed in God. She looked him in the eye and answered yes. He asked her why, but before she could answer he pulled the trigger. On that day Rachel learned that commitment had a cost. She also proved by laying down her life that she was willing to pay it. Exactly one year before, to the day, Rachel wrote the following words in her journal about commitment: "I am not going to hide the light that God has put into me. If I have to sacrifice everything, I will."

Commitment requires a willingness to sacrifice. Commitments to marriage and family are noble, but the greatest and best commitment is to God.

STEP 16

LOOK FOR LESSONS

God taught me another lesson today.

A large man with a long scruffy beard and a loud, demanding voice came into my office. His hair was uncombed, his shirt smelled of heavy sweat, and his muddy shoes left tracks across my carpet. I was put off by Tim's arrogant swagger and his order to fix his wife or I'd be sorry. But as we talked, a tear trickled down his cheek when he told me how much he loved his wife and how he was fearful she might leave him. This man who at first appeared hard-hearted was actually quite caring and tender. The longer we talked, the more I liked Tim. But I had to get past my first impression.

After Tim left, I thought of the story of Samuel looking for a king, and God says, "The Lord does not look at the things man looks at. Man looks at the outward appearance, but the Lord looks at the heart."[1] This morning God used Tim to teach me to look beyond the surface and not jump to conclusions. I learned that things are not always as they seem. It's a simple lesson—one I already knew but desperately needed to be reminded of.

Each and every day God teaches me a lesson—frequently many lessons. Some are new and enlightening, and others are reminders of things I had forgotten or had not focused on recently. Some lessons have a heavy impact; others are small and seemingly less significant. Lessons come to us in hundreds of different ways. Yet if we are not keenly attentive, we miss them. In fact, I probably miss most of what God wants to teach me. If God were to send me a hundred lessons in a day, and I were to get just one of them, I would consider myself blessed. However, I get so distracted by things like a lack of faith, bad habits, laziness, shortsightedness, immaturity, emotions, stubbornness, and exhaustion. Looking for lessons requires the intentional determination to get beyond these and whatever other distractions we may face. Yet to find these lessons we must be willing to pay attention, dig deep, and work hard. We don't appreciate what we have found if it is too easy. As Malcolm Muggeridge wrote, "Every happening, great or small, is a parable whereby God speaks to us, and the art of life is to get the message."

Learning can be an unquenchable thirst, for something new and intriguing is always right before us. As Annie Dillard reminds us, "The days tumble with meanings." Sheldon Kopp agrees when he writes in *Even a Stone Can Be a Teacher*, "Unexpected opportunities for enlightenment appear everywhere." Yet to catch the opportunities, the mind must be ready and nimble. Leonardo da Vinci warns us that "iron rusts from disuse; stagnant water loses its purity and in cold weather becomes frozen; even so does inaction sap the vigor of the mind." Too many of us have a rusty or frozen mind. Our preconceived notions keep us from growing and learning what life is really all about.

On the surface, life may look random and confusing, but that is frequently because we do not really look and we do not really think. Thinking means connecting things. It involves looking for meaning and wisdom in all we encounter. As a psychologist, I look beyond the obvious to find meaning in my clients' choice of words, facial expressions, style of dress, body language, and a thousand other factors. I look for patterns and purpose in what most might consider random things. Mathematicians find meaning in numbers and algebraic equations. Microbiologists find meaning beneath a microscope. Geologists find meaning in rocks and minerals. There is an order in this universe—an order that provides meaning and millions of amazing lessons. All we have to do is reach out and grab them.

LESSONS IN THE ORDINARY

A poor African farmer worked his land from dawn until dusk each day, barely eking out an existence. In the evenings he heard strange and wonderful stories about great diamonds from travelers passing through—diamonds found beside roads and creek beds. The more he heard of the great riches just waiting for someone to bend down and pick them up, the more excited he became.

One day he sold his farm and went out in search of the diamonds. For years he searched the African landscape, but he found nothing. Eventually he went completely broke, lost all hope, and drowned himself in a shallow river.

Meanwhile, the man who bought his farm faithfully worked his land. After a typical hard day, he picked up an unusual looking rock and took it home. Several days later a visitor saw the rock on the farmer's mantel and asked him about it.

"There are hundreds of these rocks all over my fields," said the farmer. "This one just has a unique shape."

"Don't you see what you have?" asked the visitor. "This is a diamond."

Sure enough, the original farmer had been standing on acres of diamonds, but he never saw what was right before his eyes. He sold one of the richest diamond mines in the world for just a few hundred dollars. Yet this farmer is like many of us. We miss the lessons right in front of us and go off in search of truth somewhere else.

The ordinary is only ordinary because we have grown used to it. The common, the simple, and the small often hold powerful lessons. Grace Noll Crowell wrote, "The common tasks are beautiful, if we have eyes to see their shining ministry." Laura Ingalls Wilder, author of the *Little House on the Prairie* books, put it this way: "I am beginning to learn that it is the sweet, simple things of life which are the real ones after all." Yes, it is frequently the things we ignore that can teach us the most. They are the diamonds at our feet.

So don't ignore the little things; don't label anything as insignificant or meaningless. We miss so much that happens around us. In the book of Proverbs, the writer finds wisdom in little animals he observes on an afternoon stroll. He writes about "ants—they aren't strong, but they store up food all summer" and "lizards—they are easy to catch, but they are found even in kings' palaces."[2]

Life's lessons are infinite. In *Letters to Malcolm*, C. S. Lewis writes, "Any patch of sunlight in a wood will show you something about the sun that you could never get from reading books on astronomy. These pure and spontaneous pleasures are 'patches of Godlight' in the woods of our experience." So look for lessons everywhere. You can find them in the most wonderful and surprising places: in a song or a movie, on the bumper of a car, in a dream, in a smile, on an afternoon stroll, or even in a patch of sunlight.

LESSONS IN ADVERSITY

God sometimes teaches us our best lessons through adversity. In fact, the New Testament author James refers to adversity as an opportunity. He writes that it has at least seven benefits:

1. It tests our faith.
2. It stretches our endurance.
3. It builds our character.
4. It teaches us wisdom.
5. It forces us to pray.
6. It reminds us of what really matters.
7. It brings God's blessing.

Trials, troubles, failures, mistakes, and difficulties stretch us in ways that success cannot. Adversity is a powerful teacher. In *A Better Way to Live,* Og Mandino writes, "Stars may be seen from the bottom of a deep well, when they cannot be discerned from the mountaintop. So will you learn things in adversity that you would never have discovered without trouble." It's interesting to note how many great people have experienced great adversity. George Washington's father died when George was only eleven. Abraham Lincoln's mother died when he was ten. Helen Keller was blind, and Ludwig van Beethoven was deaf. John Bunyan, author of *The Pilgrim's Progress,* spent years in prison. Walt Disney went bankrupt, and Franklin D. Roosevelt was crippled by polio. Yet, through their adversities, each of these people grew braver and stronger. In fact, these very difficulties are part of what shaped them for greatness.

If life is a test, adversities are the hardest questions. Thomas Edison spent years trying to develop a lightbulb, but failure and frustration were his main discoveries. One day he was asked if he was ready to give up. "No," was his response, "I am now well informed on six thousand ways you cannot do it." Thomas Edison found lessons in his failures, and those failures ultimately led him to success. Pat Williams, senior vice president of the Orlando Magic, wrote, "Your toughest crises are your best opportunities." Adversity is where the greatest lessons take place and truest growth forces its roots deep into your life.

In the mid-1960s Howard Rutledge, a United States Navy pilot, was shot down over North Vietnam. During his years as a prisoner of war, he was surrounded by death. Through starvation, torture, and solitary confinement he learned many lessons. In his book In the Presence of Mine Enemies, he writes, "It took prison to show me how empty life is without God." Willa Cather said it this way: "There are some things you learn best in calm, and some in storm."

LESSONS IN PEOPLE

"I met the rudest lady today," said Kristin. "I couldn't believe what she said to me. I'd never say that sort of thing to anyone. It was such a great lesson."

God brings certain people into your life at certain times with certain words and actions—all to teach you something. Every day I learn amazing things from people. I watch what they do and listen to their stories. I absorb their experiences, their successes, and failures. Today I learned about patience from Emily, commitment from Al, and the importance of going out of your way from a blind man.

Walking down the sidewalk to a local deli, I saw a man in his thirties with a white cane trying to find his way around a long hedge. I thought about helping, but I was late, and I knew he would sooner or later realize he needed to turn around and go the opposite direction.

Returning to my office with an afternoon snack, I saw the man again. He was trying to open the door of a shop that had recently gone out of business. "Can I help you?" I asked.

"I think I'm lost," he said. "I'm looking for Mervyn's Department Store."

I explained that to get to Mervyn's you must go up a half block, turn left and go three blocks, turn left again, and go an additional two blocks, then you'd find it on your right. The man looked confused, so I explained again. He thanked me and hesitantly walked forward.

"Wait a minute," I called. "Why don't I walk you there?"

Suddenly a large smile crossed his face, "Are you sure you wouldn't mind?"

"Not at all," I replied as I gave him my arm.

Later, I sat at my desk thinking, It sure feels good to help others. Now that's a great lesson that I hope I never forget.

Every person we meet has a story to tell and a lesson to teach. We are surrounded by teachers—wise senior citizens, innocent children, close friends, complete strangers, even enemies and critics. All we have to do is look and listen. Much of what I know is from listening to people's experiences. I learn from what they have learned. I borrow their discoveries and note their mistakes. I memorize what brought them success and do my best to avoid what caused them difficulties. These types of lessons are invaluable.

LESSONS IN THE PAST

As a child I could listen for hours to the stories my grandparents told about "the good old days." Their words opened up another world, full of excitement and wisdom. I heard compelling tales about the importance of honesty, loyalty, risk, hard work, and compassion. As I sat wide-eyed, they recounted real-life incidents that I still vividly recall years later. I am drawn to stories of the past. They often seem sharper and more powerful than the present. They paint a picture of the truth, which makes their lessons easier for me to grasp and remember.

An individual's personal experience is an important teacher. People who do not learn from their past are prone to repeat their mistakes and failures. We all have done and said things that, if we could live life over, we would do differently. Those who refuse to learn trap themselves and block their growth.

Driving in icy weather makes me nervous. As a teenager I got in three automobile accidents—all in icy weather. Through these three experiences I learned a number of things about slippery roads, such as don't drive under these conditions unless you have to, drive slowly, and don't slam on the brakes.

Maturity involves building on past experiences (traumas, interactions, achievements, and observations). What I do and say today is based on the lesson I learned or didn't learn yesterday. Time gives me perspective and clarity. Things I once wasn't even aware of or thought were insignificant might now become the most important of all lessons.

History is full of incredible lessons. The Bible teaches me about the lives of Abraham, Moses, Joshua, Rahab, Ruth, David, and Hosea, to name just a few. From them I learn invaluable lessons, but one of my favorites is Esther, who acted so courageously, holding firm to her belief that God was in control. When I read Esther's story, I learn that God places people in perfect positions at the perfect time in order to do his perfect purpose. I love Mordecai's words to Esther: "And who knows but that you have come to royal position for such a time as this?"[3] What a great lesson for us all. I also enjoy reading biographies. Here I discover what others learned and how they applied that knowledge to their lives. In the past year I have read stories about George Washington, John Adams, G. K. Chesterton, Mahatma Gandhi, Billy Graham, Annie Dillard, John Nash, and others. For a time, each of these became my mentor. The past is rich with wisdom and its lessons. I want as many of these teachers as possible, for it is through them that I grow deeper and stronger.

LESSONS IN GOD

I once heard a story about a young man who went on a long journey with St. Peter. One night the two came upon the simple cottage of a very poor couple whose prize possession was a cow. The humble couple welcomed them, emptied their cupboards to give them a hearty meal, and slept on the floor so St. Peter could have the best bed in their house. As St. Peter and the young man left the next morning, the poor couple's cow died.

Several days later the travelers came to the grand house of a wealthy nobleman. This man was cold and arrogant. He would hardly speak to his guests. He gave the men bread and water, then sent them to the barns to sleep with the goats. The next morning as the travelers were leaving, God told St. Peter to pay a worker to repair a wall that was falling down on the edge of the nobleman's estate.

As the two travelers were walking down the road, the young man asked St. Peter why God had punished the good couple by killing their cow and rewarded the hard-hearted nobleman by repairing his wall.

St. Peter thought for a moment and said, "You do well to ask this question, for there is a lesson in all things, but the lesson is not always obvious. The poor man's wife was set to die that morning, but because of his kindness God chose to take his cow instead. Where the nobleman's wall was falling down there is a great treasure. By repairing the wall, the nobleman will never find the treasure."

To see God's hand we must look beyond the obvious. Just as all things hold a lesson from God, so God's signature can be found in every lesson. Yet too often we only see the obvious and nothing more. We are like the people the prophet Isaiah describes when he says, "They will not see with their eyes, nor hear with their ears, nor understand with their hearts."[4] We are surrounded by God—he is so obvious, yet so hidden. Perhaps Tennessee Williams was right when he wrote, "Snatching the eternal out of the desperately fleeting is the great magic trick of human existence."

God is constantly before us. Yet we must follow Paul's guidance by fixing "our eyes not on what is seen, but on what is unseen."[5] Then we can fully understand the words of Elizabeth Barrett Browning when she wrote: "Earth's crammed with heaven, and every common bush afire with God; but only he who sees, takes off his shoes, the rest sit round it and pluck blackberries." On those days I take off my shoes and catch a glimpse of God, I am changed. I wish to spend more days aware of

- his presence—with its purity and awe;

- his hand—with its protection and comfort;

- his fist—with its power and control;

- his face—with its beauty and majesty;

- his mind—with its wisdom and direction;

- his heart—with its gentleness and love;

- his breath—with its life and creativity.

As I focus on God—opening my heart to all he is and all he does—I become keenly aware of his awesome presence. I see and hear and feel his presence everywhere. My openness invites him to come near and fill me with his peace. I want to be like the woman who reached out to touch Jesus, even if it was just the edge of his coat, and was suddenly filled with his power.[6]

Yet, if I close myself to his lessons, I am closing myself to him. At that point, I stop growing, and the abundant life slips through my fingers. God waits patiently, allowing me to surround myself with darkness. But he still waits, giving me more chances to reach out and see him. Yet, what if I refuse to stretch out my hand or open wide my eyes? Then with deep sadness, I believe, he retreats, and I am left alone. That is perhaps the most tragic lesson of all: If we refuse him, he lets us go. Please don't let this happen to you.

A thousand lessons stand before you in a thousand different forms. Some are obvious, and some are not. Open your eyes, your ears, your heart. Let your soul always stand ajar—seeking, waiting, welcoming the next lesson. And each evening as you turn out the light and let your head sink into the pillow, review the events of the day. Search for lessons that God has placed along your way—all those messages, both grand or simple, which are easily lost in the rush and clutter, could make your life much more meaningful.

STEP 17
ACCEPT MYSTERY

John Nash Jr. was the most creative and brilliant mathematician in the last half of the twentieth century. At age nineteen he was considered a genius by his professors. At twenty-one he started solving the most complex and perplexing problems in modern mathematics—problems that later earned him the 1994 Nobel Prize in economics. Breakthrough after breakthrough shocked the best minds in the world. At twenty-five he proved the "isometric embeddability of abstract Riemannian manifolds in Euclidean spaces"; nothing seemed beyond the intellectual grasp of this amazing young man. Yet at age twenty-nine, he was struck by paranoid schizophrenia and was soon unable to compose a logical sentence or take care of his own basic needs.

What drove John Nash Jr. to a complete mental breakdown? He believed it was because he was trying to solve one of the greatest mathematical mysteries of all time, what many called the "holy grail of pure mathematics." The intellectual and emotional force required to challenge this mystery ultimately broke him for the next twenty-five years.

It is important to pay attention, dig deep, and look for lessons, but it is just as important to accept mystery. Every problem cannot be solved, nor every situation understood. The Talmud says, "Accustom your tongue to say, 'I don't know.'" There is much we don't know, and that is okay.

The older I get, the easier it is for me to embrace mystery. Many of the carefully constructed boxes I held to when I was younger no longer hold up to intellectual scrutiny. I don't know as much as I thought I did. I have learned to enjoy the puzzles of life. I have come to relax with obscurity and ambiguity. I live with hundreds of curious paradoxes and thousands of unanswered questions. All these things used to keep me up at night, but now I have given up on figuring it all out. By no means does this mean I have become passive or that my hyperactive curiosity has diminished one iota. It simply means I am at peace with mystery. At times I even cherish it.

Accepting mystery involves embracing that childlike awe and wonder that adulthood seems to steal from us. Maybe this is what Albert Einstein meant when he wrote, "Do not grow old, no matter how long you live. Never cease to stand like curious children before the great mystery into which we were born." Mystery involves excitement and adventure and surprise. What a wonderful way to live. In fact, a life without those qualities is hardly worth living. I have to agree with Harry Emerson Fosdick when he wrote, "I would rather live in a world where my life is surrounded by mystery than live in a world so small that my mind could comprehend it." So let mystery have its place in you.

LIFE AND MYSTERY

Everyday life is full of mysteries to pursue. I love what Frederich Buechner writes in *Now and Then*: "Listen to your life. See it for the fathomless mystery that it is." This is a journey of unanswered questions, riddles, wonders, enigmas, and incomprehensibilities. The most common and ordinary aspects of life are embedded with mystery. As I ponder this concept on a cloudy day, here are a few of the mysteries that awe and baffle me:

- conception and birth

- the functioning of the human brain

- the character of light

- good and evil

- romantic love

- stars and outer space

- the complexity and simplicity of nature

- order in the midst of chaos

Annie Dillard wrote, "Our life is a faint tracing on the surface of mystery." The mysteries of life both woo and terrify. Frederick Buechner wrote that God provides us all with "momentary glimpses into a mystery of such depth, power, and beauty that if we were to see it head on, in any other way than in glimpses, I suspect we would be annihilated." Too much mystery undoes us; too little mystery denies us. William Blake embraced mystery and in so doing saw life at a deeper level. Therefore, he encouraged all "to see a world in a grain of sand and a heaven in an hour."

In order to see the multitude of mysteries that daily surrounds us, we must learn to value all that creation holds. For when we value something, we are forced to look at it a little closer. And as we look closer at the beauty and the intricacies of this life, we can't help but be struck with a certain enchantment. It may seem so simple at first glance, but as you continue to gaze at the world around you, your appreciation will be amplified, and the mysterious will leave you stunned and surprised. As Fyodor Dostoyevsky teaches in his masterpiece, *The Brothers Karamazov*, "Love all God's creations, the whole and every grain of sand in it. Love every leaf, every ray of God's light. . . . If you love everything, you will perceive the divine mystery in things." Therefore accepting mystery becomes one of the most joyful and mind stretching of all activities.

This is a marvelous world of magic and mystery. Yet too often we rationalize the magic and fear the mystery. What a terrible shame! It is the mystery of life that makes its adventure so glorious and enticing. The best things in life are the most embedded with mystery, which makes the journey all the more joyful to those who are willing to celebrate the unsolvable and incalculable. One of the most joyful of all writers was G. K. Chesterton. He reveled in mystery and in *Orthodoxy* wrote, "We all feel the riddle of the earth without anyone to point it out. The mystery of life is the plainest part of it. . . . Every stone or flower is a hieroglyphic of which we have lost the key; with every step of our lives we enter into the middle of some story which we are certain to misunderstand." So much mystery, and so much we don't understand. How amazing! As I grow older and wiser, the mystery of life seems to expand rather than shrink. Yet this is good, and this seems to be as it should. So as we grow accustomed to mystery, we'll learn that life's greatest mysteries are really God's mysteries.

THE MYSTERY OF GOD

God is a mystery, and the life he gives us is a mystery. St. Augustine described God as "most hidden, yet most present." Even what we think we understand about God, we don't. Like the apostle Paul says, "Now we see things imperfectly as in a cloudy mirror. . . . All that I know now is partial and incomplete."[1] No matter how hard we strain our eyes, our view of God is dim and hazy and indistinct. God is infinite in terms of time, space, presence, knowledge, power, perfection, love, goodness, wisdom, justice, and all other things. He is so close we can't focus on him and yet so far away that we can barely see him. In spite of our incredible limitations, God edges into our lives in a thousand different ways.

God's ways stretch us beyond our limits. How can we explain the ways of one so mysterious? The best we can do is to make simple guesses as to the mind of the Almighty. "My ways are far beyond anything you could imagine. For just as the heavens are higher than the earth, so my ways are higher than your ways."[2] As an ant contemplates the Statue of Liberty or the Golden Gate Bridge, so we reflect on God. St. Teresa of Avila put it simply, "Blessed are those in awe of God." What else can our response be? Yet for the ordinary seeker of God, maybe Jonathan Edwards was right when he preached, "Were God to disclose but a little of that which is seen by saints and angels in heaven, our frail natures would sink under it."

This world is full of paradoxes and mystery. Why should it surprise us that the maker of this world is also full of paradoxes and mystery? God is mystery, and he is the heart of the universe. The apostle Paul reminds us that "he existed before anything else, and he holds all creation together."[3] Not only does he hold all creation together, but he is beyond all creation. Solomon declared, "Even the highest heavens cannot contain you."[4] God is beyond all things. Nothing can constrain him or limit him.

It all comes down to this: God is so great, and we are so small. Our arrogance and selfishness tempt us to imagine we're bigger than we really are. Our faith tells us to face reality and accept our limitations. Faith involves not fighting with God about the facts. It's accepting that some things don't make sense to us but knowing that they ultimately work out to God's best. In *The Signature of Jesus*, Brennan Manning writes that faith "is movement into obscurity, into the undefined, into ambiguity, and not into some predetermined, clearly delineated plan for the future. Each future determination, each next step discloses itself only out of a discernment of the influence of God in the present moment." To be a person of faith sometimes involves not knowing. As we trust God, we can transform mysteries from points of anxiety or frustration to points of peace and joyfulness. As Dr. James Dobson wrote, "Our task is not to decipher exactly how all of life's pieces fit and what it all means, but to remain faithful and obedient to Him who knows all mysteries."

THE MYSTERY OF MIRACLES

God truly does work in mysterious ways. When I was in college, I drove to Prineville reservoir to go camping with a few buddies. It was very late, and I was driving faster than I should. Just before the campsite, the road curved sharply high above the reservoir. When I hit the first curve, I couldn't stay on the road. I slammed on the brakes and spun out in the gravel on the edge of the cliff, but somehow I maneuvered my way back to the road. The next morning I went back to the site to see how close to the edge I'd gotten. In shock I followed the tracks—and saw where all four tires went off the cliff. Ten feet to my left I saw where all four tires returned to the cliff. How in the world did my car go off the edge without it crashing into the reservoir below? There is no logical way this could happen. It was nothing short of a miracle. It appears that Job was right when he said to God, "I know that you can do anything, and no one can stop you."[5]

Miracles are simply those things in life that are unexpected. Dan Wakefield writes in *Expect a Miracle*, a "miracle is the realm of possibility beyond what we presently know." God isn't limited by our expectations. H. G. Wells wrote that "each moment of life is a miracle and a mystery." In our age of science and rationality, we try to explain away the miracles and mystery of life. We want control, and to accept miracles shows that we don't have control. However, we live in a spiritual universe, and we are surrounded by miracles. Every day small miracles take place before our very eyes; it is only when a larger miracle catches us by surprise that we stand back in awe. Ronald Knox wrote, "Miracles are God's signature, appended to his masterpiece of creation."

I once heard a story about a powerful storm that tore through the mountains around La Ceiba, Honduras, for three days. Yet Tito Rodrigues was determined to drive to the village. When he arrived, the people were surprised to see him.

"How did you get here?" they asked.

"I came on the main road," he replied.

"That's impossible!" they said. "The bridge was washed out last night."

Tito told them that the bridge must have already been repaired, for the wood was still white and unweathered.

"No," the people insisted, "the bridge is gone." A few of the villagers traveled back with Tito to where a thirty-foot wooden span had once crossed a deep chasm—and there was no bridge. Tito stared across the river in bewilderment. How had he just a few hours before driven across a bridge of brand-new wood that hadn't been there for three days?

We live in a universe where God does the impossible and the unimaginable. When he bewilders us, we call it a miracle. Yet these are simply God showing us his hand. As J. I. Packer wrote, "There is nothing irrational about believing that the God who made the world can still intrude creatively into it." God rules over everything, and his presence is everywhere. Sometimes this presence shines through the commonplace, but we are often too distracted to acknowledge it. Therefore, God must sometimes use the spectacular or miraculous to get our attention. C. S. Lewis described miracles as the "retelling in small letters of the very same story which is written across the whole world in letters too large for some of us to see." The real miracle is that God cares enough to even get our attention.

One of the most frequently reported forms of miracles involves angels. David Jeremiah wrote, "I'm more convinced than ever that angels are far more involved in our world than most of us realize." On a beautiful spring day a young mother looked out her kitchen window and noticed that her garden gate had been left open. She also saw that her three-year-old daughter had pushed through the gate and was calmly sitting on the railroad tracks playing with the gravel. The mother panicked as she saw a train speeding down the tracks toward her precious daughter. Racing from the house, she saw a beautiful, pure-white figure lift her daughter off the tracks just as the train rushed by. Then the shining form stood alongside the track with an arm around the child. When the mother reached her daughter, the three-year-old was standing alone. This is just one of millions of true stories involving the interaction of angels in our everyday life. Probably you or someone you know has a similar story. Only the most jaded or skeptical would deny the mystery of the miracle of angels.

There is so much we don't understand, but that is what stretches our faith. Pam Reeve defines faith as "living with the unexplained." I would take it one step further and say that authentic faith embraces mystery. Mystery is like a window through which we may look beyond the walls of this world. Yet what we see when we open our spiritual eyes is unclear, incomplete, paradoxical, and confusing. That is the very nature of mystery. L. Frank Baum, the author of *The Wizard of Oz*, wrote, "Never question the truth of what you fail to understand, for the world is filled with wonders." As we accept mystery, Anton Chekhov, the Russian playwright, wrote, "we shall find peace. We shall hear angels, We shall see the sky sparkling with diamonds." To believe we can or should understand all things is to deprive ourselves of the opportunities offered by plunging deeply into the life of faith. Accepting and relaxing in mystery allows peace to sink deeply into every aspect of our life. As Socrates once said, "You will be gentler and more agreeable to your companions, having the good sense not to fancy you know what you do not know."

STEP ⑱

SHINE BRIGHTLY

As George Bailey stood on the bridge and stared into the icy water, he felt that his life was a failure. It was Christmas Eve, and he believed that this world would be better without him. George had been an example of light in a dark world, but he felt as if it was a wasted effort. At this crucial moment Clarence, an angel trying to earn his wings, shows George what his hometown of Bedford Falls would have been like without his good example and positive influence. His brother would have died because George wasn't there to save him. His wife would have been a lonely spinster, and the greedy Mr. Potter would have destroyed all that was good in the town.

"One man's life touches so many others," Clarence tells George. "When he's not there, it leaves an awfully big hole."

It's a Wonderful Life has become a holiday classic and one of the most beloved films of all time. Its lesson is timeless: Shine brightly. Be a candle in the darkness. Jesus says, "You are the light of the world—like a city on a hilltop that cannot be hidden. No one lights a lamp and then puts it under a basket. Instead, a lamp is placed on a stand, where it gives light to everyone in the house."[1] George Bailey learned that he made a difference, and that in a hundred different ways his light had pushed back the darkness. Edward Everett Hale wrote, "I am only one, but I am one. I cannot do everything, but I can do something. And I will not let what I cannot do interfere with what I can do." Every person has influence, and yours is probably much bigger than you will ever realize. You may only be a small spark of light, but you can make a big difference. Stop for a moment and consider who has shined brightly for you:

- A parent who believed in you

- A teacher who challenged you

- A coach who motivated you

- A friend who stood beside you

- A colleague who encouraged you

- A writer who opened ideas to you

- A hero whose story inspired you

You can have the same influence—so use it. William James wrote, "Act as if what you do makes a difference. It does."

THE POWER OF EXAMPLE

I was at a local grocery store picking up some milk and bread when a large, muscular police officer approached me. Before I could say anything, he wrapped his arms around me and gave me a powerful hug. He must have sensed my shock and confusion, for he said, "You don't recognize me, do you? I'm Ryan."

I had last seen Ryan twelve years earlier. He'd been a depressed, insecure teenager who had made a few poor decisions, but he had a dream. We had talked no more than ten times during a six-month period. Mostly I just listened and encouraged him to think before he acted.

"Thank you, Dr. Steve," he said. "You were the only one who believed in me. I wanted to be a cop, and everybody thought I was crazy. But you said that I'd be a great cop. I never forgot your words. Now look at me."

I looked at the handsome young man in his spotless uniform. His confidence and joy inspired me. He showed me pictures of his wife and two small children. He told me how he works with teenagers in his church, encouraging them to be all that God wants them to be. This young man shone brightly. He reminded me of what King Solomon said: "The way of the righteous is like the first gleam of dawn, which shines ever brighter until the full light of day."[2]

As one small candle shines alone in the darkness, it can light another, which lights another—until our corner of the world is ablaze with brightness. Norman B. Rice wrote, "Dare to reach out your hand into the darkness, to pull another hand into the light." It doesn't take a lot to brighten your world—a positive word, a simple smile, a good deed. Let no one encounter you without your parting gift of encouragement and hope. President Woodrow Wilson said, "You are not here merely to make a living. You are here in order to enable the world to live more amply, with greater vision, with a finer spirit of hope and achievement. You are here to enrich the world, and you impoverish yourself if you forget the errand." To shine brightly is to intentionally stand boldly against the darkness. Boris Yeltsin said it this way: "A man must live like a great brilliant flame and burn as brightly as he can." As we shine brightly, we make a path for others. Through our example we give them a light to find their way. Albert Schweitzer said, "Example is not the main thing in influencing others. It is the only thing." Words of advice might be helpful and powerful, but I have come to believe that people are changed more by the light of example than by anything else.

LIGHTING OUR WORLD

Light is a marvelous thing. Without it we would live sad and limited lives, but with it we are capable of almost anything. When all is dark, we grow cold and confused; we get lost and stumble; we become fearful and anxious. The first chapter of Genesis says, "The earth was formless . . . and darkness covered the deep waters. . . . Then God said, 'Let there be light,' and there was light. And God saw that the light was good."[3] Light wakes us up, ignites us, and energizes us. Light gives us life. It chases away the darkness and opens up a world of possibilities. To bring light into our world is to change everything. Here are eight aspects of light that can make all the difference in our lives and possibly in our world.

Light is truth: Darkness and shadows hide the truth, potentially creating confusion, distortion, misunderstanding, and crisis. But the brighter the light, the clearer the truth. To shine brightly we must hold to the truth, even when it is tough and uncomfortable. Let your light be true and trustworthy. This will draw others to you. Margaret Fuller wrote, "If you have knowledge, let others light their candles at it." Truth and knowledge provide credibility, but they must always be tempered with wisdom. Daniel wrote, "Those who are wise will shine as bright as the sky."[4]

Light is vision: Without light we cannot see; we are blind to all that is around us. Vision provides clarity, purpose, and direction. Solomon wrote, "Where there is no vision, the people perish."[5] Vision shows you where you are going, and as Ralph Waldo Emerson said, "The world makes way for the man who knows where he is going." Light guides and directs you like a beacon on a rocky shore—guiding you away from danger and directing you toward a safe harbor. Gary Collins wrote, "When vision fades, passion cools, enthusiasm dissipates, indecision and inertia take over and hope disappears."

Light is warmth: Bright, sunny days energize me. Cold, cloudy days cause me to bundle up and retreat. Similarly, I am drawn to the light and warmth of a blazing campfire. Light warms me up physically, emotionally, and socially. A smile, a hug, a compliment, a positive attitude, a simple gift, or an encouraging conversation can also provide a light that warms me through and through. Lucy Laviom encourages us all: "If the world seems cold to you, kindle fires to keep warm."

Light is joy: When most people smile, really smile, their eyes sparkle. When someone is filled with joy, it seems to shine through their eyes. In fact, the Hebrew word for joy has the root meaning "to shine" or "to be bright." King David wrote, "Weeping may last through the night, but joy comes with the morning."[6] As the sun breaks above the horizon, chasing away the darkness, there is joy. You see the beauty, the excitement, the entrance of a new day, and fresh opportunities. When things are dark, we become more serious and somber. Yet when things are bright and filled with light, joy sweeps over us.

Light is courage: As a child I was afraid of the dark. I could imagine some terrifying evil or dangerous monster lurking in the darkness. Yet all my mother had to do was turn on a light, and all was safe. As an adult, I'm aware that the darkness of fear can still grip me. Jim Wallis, editor-in-chief of *Sojourners* magazine, wrote, "We need the light of courage to face the darkness that lies so thick and heavy before us." Norman Macleod wrote, "Courage, brother, do not stumble, though thy path be dark as night: there is a star to guide the humble." That star is God, for as John wrote, "God is light."[7] With the light of God brightening my heart and guiding my path, I shall fear no darkness.

Light is character: Living a good life of love, generosity, and kindness is to be a light in a world of greed and selfishness. Shakespeare writes in *The Merchant of Venice*: "How far that little candle throws his beams! So shines a good deed in a naughty world." The darker the night, the brighter the light. The apostle Paul encourages us to "live as children of light."[8] We need to be a candle, a campfire, a lighthouse, anything to chase away the darkness. John Winthrop, the first governor of the Massachusetts Bay Colony, said in 1630, "We shall be as a city on a hill; the eyes of all people are upon us." To let my character shine bright I do all I can to "hate what is evil; cling to what is good."[9] D. L. Moody said it this way: "A holy life will produce the deepest impression. Lighthouses blow no horns; they only shine."

Light is hope: Without hope, we are lost and forced into despair. Situations might sometimes appear hopeless, but with God there is always hope. In his letter to the church at Ephesus, Paul writes, "I pray that your hearts will be flooded with light so that you can understand the confident hope he has given to those he called."[10] Disappointments and frustrations are limited and temporary. Beyond them, there is always hope—shining brightly and boldly, calling us forward.

Light is faith: Faith is the spotlight that shines through the darkness. It is the greatest light. Chuck Swindoll wrote that with faith "there's no barrier too high, no valley too deep, no dream too extreme, no challenge too great." With faith, all things are possible. Faith allows us to shine. Isaiah wrote that those with faith "will find new strength. They will soar high on wings like eagles. They will run and not grow weary. They will walk and not faint."[11] Faith is the light that ignites us, fuels us, and keeps us burning.

SHINE YOUR LIGHT

Each of us is like a candle. Many have never been lit or have been blown out. Others are a mere spark or are flickering desperately to keep burning. Only a few shine brightly enough to light their world and pass that light to others.

It's been said that a thousand candles can be lit from a single flame, but that flame must be bold. Someone once asked Malcolm Muggeridge what he most wanted to do with the rest of his life. His answer was, "I should like my light to shine, even if only very fitfully, like a match struck in a dark, cavernous night." My wish would be the same. When I was a child one of my favorite songs had the simple lyrics: "This little light of mine, I'm going to let it shine."

In a world of darkness, light makes a large difference. People yearn for light, even if they may squint when they see it. I want to be a light shining brightly. But to shine takes more than just well-intentioned words. Don't just talk about light, produce some. Charles Spurgeon wrote that good intentions must be seen: "Lamps do not talk, but they do shine." St. Francis of Assisi summarizes it all in his famous prayer when he cried out, "Where there is darkness, let me give light." And this light will change the world. In a speech Nelson Mandela reminded us all that "as we let our own light shine, we unconsciously give other people permission to do the same."

Two of the men I admire the most lived a hundred years apart and were born several hundred miles apart. One was a white military commander, and the other was a black man of peace. Yet both were men of faith and courage. They both shone brightly with incredible light, vision, and warmth.

Robert E. Lee, the commander of the Confederate army in the Civil War, was a model of love. He respected his men and took every opportunity to show compassion. Shortly after the war ended General Lee was attending a church service in Richmond, Virginia. When Communion was served, a black man walked up the aisle to take the bread and cup. An angry murmur swept across the white congregation as they saw this former slave at the front of their church. The mood was blatantly hostile and distinctly cold. But Robert E. Lee rose to his feet, walked forward, and knelt beside the black man. The two shared the cup and received Communion together. The church was silent, with everybody staring in confusion. The general turned to the congregation and simply said, "All men are brothers in Christ." The coldness broke, and soon the rest of the congregation stepped forward to take Communion.

Dr. Martin Luther King Jr. was another man who shined brightly. As a leader of the civil rights movement, he was beaten, kicked, and had eggs and rocks thrown at him. He was spit at, thrown into jail, humiliated, and received death threats, but he refused to retaliate. In January 1956 his house was bombed, and a violent mob gathered seeking revenge. Dr. King spoke to the crowd, saying, "My wife and baby are all right. I want you to put down your weapons and go home. . . . Remember what the Bible tells us: 'Do not be overcome by evil, but overcome evil with good.'"

No matter how unfairly treated or abused, Dr. King was consistent in his words and actions. In a later speech he said, "Do to us what you will, we will still love you. . . . And so throw us in jail, and we will still love you. Bomb our homes and threaten our children, and we will still love you. Send your hooded perpetrators of violence into our communities at the midnight hours, and drag us out on some wayside road and beat us and leave us half dead; and as difficult as it is, we will still love you."

In 1964 Dr. King was awarded the Nobel Peace Prize. He continued to speak his message of love and nonviolent resistance right to his death. On April 4, 1968, he was shot down in Memphis, Tennessee, as he stepped onto the balcony of the Lorraine Motel. Years earlier, he'd been asked how he would like to be remembered. He replied that when people mentioned his name, he hoped they'd think that he "gave his life serving others, that he tried to love people, that he tried to feed the hungry, that he tried to clothe those who were naked, that he tried to visit those who were in prison, that he tried to love and serve humanity."

These two men are brightly shining lights in my life. Among many others, they have helped influence and encourage me so that I might be a light that can in some small way influence and encourage others. In so doing, I pray that others may in turn ignite light within their sphere until someday we together can push back the darkness and live in the glorious light of God's goodness.

STEP ⑲
NURTURE PEACE

Long ago a noble king offered a great treasure to the artist in his kingdom who could paint the picture that best portrayed the meaning of peace. Hundreds of artists accepted the challenge, and within several months, paintings began to arrive at the royal castle. Special judges carefully evaluated each painting, and soon the three best were set aside for the king's judgment.

The first picture showed a perfectly clear lake. Reflected on its surface were the surrounding majestic, snowcapped mountains. The sky was a beautiful blue with a single fluffy white cloud.

The second picture depicted a young mother standing in a gentle meadow sprinkled with white and yellow wildflowers. In the mother's arms was a sleeping baby, carefully wrapped in a pure-white blanket. The mother gazed into the baby's face with tender, loving care.

The third picture showed a stark and treacherous mountain beneath an angry sky of black, evil-looking clouds. Rain fell and lightning flashed. Down the side of the mountain a waterfall cascaded onto a mass of rugged rocks.

After careful consideration, the king chose the artist of the third painting to win the great treasure. Many of the people of the kingdom were surprised by this choice, but upon a closer examination they understood the king's wisdom. For behind the churning waterfall was painted a small, scraggly bush growing out of a crack in the rock. In the bush a mother bird had built a nest. And there, surrounded by stormy weather and turbulent water, sat the mother bird on her nest—in perfect peace.

True peace involves a calm heart, even when everything around us is in turmoil. My dictionary defines *peace* as "a state of quiet or tranquillity;

freedom from disturbance or agitation." Yet we live in a world of noise and agitation. We race about and fill every moment of our day. We worry and feel stressed out and are surrounded by turmoil. A thousand things, real and imagined, seem determined to steal our peace. Yet we all dream of this elusive state of tranquillity. Joseph Conrad, the novelist, wrote, "I take it that what all men are really after is some form or . . . formula of peace." We need peace, for it frees us from worry and allows us to concentrate on what's most important. It gives us a better quality of life as well as a longer life.

People watching is an informative hobby. People are so interesting; their actions, tone of voice, and body language can tell you so much about them. I can observe a person's level of peace by simply watching his or her face—eyes, mouth, forehead. As I'm writing this I'm at the San Francisco International Airport, watching masses of people rush about anxiously trying to catch their next flight. A gray-haired man in a business suit looks terribly upset as he argues angrily with the ticket agent. His eyes dart back and forth, his brow is furrowed, and a blood vessel bulges at his temple. A twenty-something mother, sitting beside her daughter, is lost in thought. Her eyes are unfocused, a frown creases her mouth, and her jaw is tense. There is no peace in either of these faces. As I watch people, I wonder whether there is any peace on earth.

In spite of all the conflict, turmoil, trouble, and anxiety of this world, true peace, though rare, is definitely possible. Peace is one of the most treasured and sought-after gifts one can possess. Pope John XXIII said, "A peaceful man does more good than a learned man." In fact, a learned man without peace is miserable. Genuine peace must come from above. Moses said, "May the Lord show you his favor and give you his peace."[1] Jesus said, "I am leaving you with a gift—peace of mind and heart. And the peace I give is a gift the world cannot give."[2] Ultimately, peace comes from the knowledge that God has overcome and that our troubles here are temporary.

As we live peacefully and nurture peace, we must deal with it on three different levels: peace with ourselves, peace with others, and peace with God. As we do this, we can pray with St. Francis of Assisi, "Lord, make me an instrument of your peace."

PEACE WITH OURSELVES

There are many aspects to nurturing our own inner peace, but it must start with simplifying and slowing down. These are flip sides of the same coin. It is difficult to simplify our lives without slowing down, and we will struggle with slowing down until we simplify. To gain inner peace, one must turn inward. Hannah Whithall Smith wrote, "Where the soul is full of peace and joy, outward surrounding and circumstances are of comparatively little account." Peace with ourselves requires letting go. Henry Miller wrote, "If there is to be any peace, it will come through being, not having." Therefore, we must remove the extra stuff that distracts, consumes, and wears us out. Hans Hoffman put it this way: "The ability to simplify means to eliminate the unnecessary so that the necessary may speak."

Yet most of us are so overwhelmed with the trivial that we have little time left for the important. Therefore we must simplify and declutter our

- emotions

- relationships

- thoughts

- schedule

- wants

- work

- expectations

- home

- words

- life

Booker T. Washington said, "There is no power on earth that can neutralize the influence of a high, simple, and useful life." This is the sort of life that brings inner peace. As we simplify, then the following words of the apostle Paul can become a reality in our life: "Let the peace that comes from Christ rule in your hearts. For . . . you are called to live in peace."[3]

Just as there is more to life than stuff and clutter, so there is more to life than speeding through each day. An old fable tells of a rabbi who saw a man running down a road and asked him, "Why do you run?" The man said he was running after his good fortune. "Foolish man," said the rabbi, "your good fortune has been chasing you for many days, but you are running too fast." So slow down; there is so much we are missing. In Lee L. Jampolsky's book *Smile for No Good Reason*, he encourages us all to slow down and

- walk in something soft with bare feet;

- eat slowly and taste your food;

- feel your heart while you smile;

- smell flowers;

- listen to water;

- watch the moon rise;

- touch a baby.

The value of slowing down is not in the individual activities but in the peace that comes as a result of doing them. Slowing down allows us to catch our breath and absorb the moment. It gives us the time to contemplate, gain perspective, and make peace. There is great value in slowing down.

Early one morning a man and his father started on a long journey into town to sell their vegetables. The son figured that if they traveled all day and night, they'd make it to the market by early the next morning. So he kept prodding the ox with a stick, urging the beast to move faster.

"Take it easy, Son," said the old man.

"If we get to the market ahead of the others, we'll get the best prices," argued the son.

Four miles down the road the father said, "Here's your uncle's place. Let's stop and say hello."

"But we've already lost an hour," complained the son.

The boy fidgeted while the two old men talked for almost an hour. On the move again they approached a fork in the road, and the father led the ox to the right.

"The left is shorter," said the son.

"But this way is so much prettier."

The winding path led through meadows, wildflowers, and along a rippling stream. But the young man churned with anxiety and didn't even notice the lovely sunset. "Let's sleep here," said the father.

"This is the last trip I'm taking with you," snapped his son. "You're more interested in watching sunsets than in making money!"

Before sunrise the young man hurriedly woke his father and headed down the road. About a mile later they happened on a stranger trying to pull his cart out of a ditch.

"Let's give him a hand," whispered the old man.

"And lose more time?" the boy exploded.

"Relax, Son. You might be in a ditch sometime yourself."

It was almost 8:00 AM by the time the other cart was back on the road. Suddenly, a brilliant flash split the sky. Beyond the hills the sky grew dark.

"Looks like big rain in the city," said the old man.

"If we had hurried, we'd be almost sold out by now," grumbled his son.

"Slow down, and you'll enjoy life so much more," said the old man.

It was late in the afternoon when they reached the hill overlooking the city. They stopped and stared down at it for a long time. Neither said a word. Finally, the young man put his hand on his father's shoulder, "I see what you mean, Dad."

They turned their cart around and began to roll slowly away from what had once been the city of Hiroshima.

By simplifying and slowing down, we open the door to inner peace. We now have the time and ability to nurture the very peace we all desire. That inner peace brings with it a gentleness and calm and contentment that radiates throughout every aspect of us. It also shines forth to anyone who comes in contact with us. Thomas à Kempis wrote, "First keep the peace within yourself, then you can also bring peace to others." Inner peace becomes outer peace. William Butler Yeats, Nobel Prize–winning poet, wrote: "We can make our minds so like still water, that beings gather about us, that they may see their own images, and so live for a moment with a clearer, perhaps even with a fiercer life because of our quiet." When we have peace with ourselves, we yearn for and facilitate peace with others.

PEACE WITH OTHERS

Self-interest, with all its variations, steals one's peace. It is as we give to others that we discover the greatest joy and peace. Aristotle said, "The greatest virtues are those that are most useful to other persons." Reaching out and serving others teaches us the power of love. Loretta Girzartis wrote, "If someone listens, or stretches out a hand, or whispers a kind word of encouragement, or attempts to understand a lonely person, extraordinary things begin to happen." As we serve others, our heart softens, our mind opens, our body relaxes, our relationships improve, and our spirit draws closer to God. Albert Schweitzer reminds us that "the only really happy people are those who have learned to serve."

To have and give peace we must intentionally look for daily opportunities to develop a servant's heart. John Wooden said, "You can't live a perfect day without doing something for someone who will never be able to repay you." These opportunities surround us in hundreds of small ways wherever we may be. In fact, they are frequently so small that we hardly pay attention to them or consider them seriously. Dietrich Bonhoeffer wrote: "Active helpfulness means, initially, simple assistance in trifling, external matters. . . . We must be ready to allow ourselves to be interrupted by God. God will be constantly crossing our paths and canceling our plans by sending us people with claims and petitions." Service might involve talking on the phone when you'd rather not, inviting someone out to lunch you don't know very well, watching a neighbor's children when you have better things to do, or loaning something to someone that might be damaged or never returned. Ralph Waldo Emerson wrote that "the best way to find yourself is to lose yourself in the service of others."

Truly great people are willing to serve. Jesus said, "Whoever wants to be a leader among you must be your servant."[4] A few days later he washed his disciples' feet. As Francis of Assisi traveled from town to town, he took a Bible and a broom—a Bible to preach the good news and a broom to sweep out the churches. Jimmy Carter, even though he was president of the

United States, serves others by teaching Sunday school, mowing the church lawn, and building houses for the underprivileged. I've heard a story about another U.S. president, Ronald Reagan. Shortly after taking office, he was shot. While in the hospital, he went to the bathroom to slap some water on his face. Some water got on the floor, so he got a few paper towels and knelt on the cold tile to clean it up. An aide came in and saw what the still very sick president was doing. The aide said, "Let the nurse deal with that." The president looked and replied, "Oh no. I made that mess, and I'd hate for the nurse to have to clean it up."

There is something great and Christlike in humble and sacrificial service to others. In *The Purpose-Driven Life,* Rick Warren writes that real servants

- make themselves available to serve;

- pay attention to needs;

- do their best with what they have.

Service is love in action. It is our best gift to each other. It is the gift of peace because love and service often soften the heart of the receiver. Jim Rohn wrote, "Whoever renders service to many puts himself in life for greatness—great wealth, great return, great satisfaction, great reputation, and great joy." And I would most certainly add: great peace.

In their book *Fearfully and Wonderfully Made,* Dr. Paul Brand and Philip Yancey tell the following story: Shortly after World War II, German students volunteered to help rebuild a cathedral in England, which had been nearly destroyed by Luftwaffe bombings. As the work progressed, they came upon a large statue of Jesus with his arms outstretched and a plaque at his feet saying, "Come unto me." Careful patching could repair all damage to the statue except for Christ's hands, which had been completely shattered by bomb fragments. The workers didn't know what to do. Finally they decided to do nothing except change the message. So even today, many years later, there stands in an English cathedral a statue of Jesus—with no hands. At his feet the plaque now reads: "Christ has no hands but ours."

True Christians do the work of Christ. Jesus said, "The Son of Man came not to be served but to serve others."[5] For as you serve others, you serve God. And his peace fills you. As Mother Teresa would frequently say, "The fruit of service is peace."

PEACE WITH GOD

True and lasting peace can come only from God. Ultimately we must all turn to our heavenly Father for peace. Dante summarized this truth in six simple words: "In His will is our peace." We must let go of our will and ego in complete surrender to God. Peace is the deliberate release of my life and all it contains to the will of God. Therefore, every moment of every day surrender yourself to his wisdom and peace. As the highly respected nineteenth-century preacher Andrew Murray wrote, "May not a single moment of my life be spent outside the light, love, and joy of God's presence and not a moment without the total surrender of myself as a vessel for him to fill full of His Spirit and His love."

Through complete surrender we discover the reality of God and the wonder of his goodness. Our surrender need not be born out of exhaustion or desperation, though it sometimes is. Surrender may also be born out of love or reason. St. Therese Couderc wrote, "Oh! If people could just understand ahead of time the sweetness and peace that are savored when nothing is held back from a good God." She later wrote: "I abandon myself sincerely to God's will and good pleasure, and when I have sincerely made this act of abandonment, I am calm and I experience a great peace."

Our natural tendency is to hold on to what is familiar and comfortable, without realizing that what God offers is so much more amazing. Thomas Kelly writes in *A Testament of Devotion* that the life surrendered to God "is astonishing in its completeness. Its joys are ravishing, its peace profound, its humility the deepest, its power world-shaking, its love enveloping, its simplicity that of a trusting child." God has awesome, exciting things in store for us if we only submit to his will. As Oswald Chambers notes in *My Utmost for His Highest*, "Once we are totally surrendered to God, He will work through us all the time." Even Jesus, as he anticipated his crucifixion, cried out to his Father, "Not my will, but thine, be done."[6]

The Lord is my peace. He calms my spirit, my heart, my mind. Woodrow Kroll affirms this when he writes, "If our minds are stayed upon God, His peace will rule the affairs entertained by our minds. If, on the other hand, we allow our minds to dwell on the cares of this world, God's peace will be far from our thoughts." Difficulties and troubles will come. They will call to us and try to overwhelm us, but they need not control us. As we surrender our heart and mind to the one in control of all, we will find an unexplainable calm in the midst of turmoil. The apostle Paul, while in jail and experiencing many challenges, wrote that God's peace "exceeds anything we can understand. His peace will guard your hearts and minds as you live in Christ Jesus."[7] This is the sort of peace that we all yearn for.

Thomas à Kempis wrote a prayer of surrender in The Imitation of Christ that many have found helpful: "Lord, You know what is best; let this be done or that be done as You please. Give what You will, as much as You will, when You will. Do with me as You know best, as will most please You, and will be for Your greater honor. Place me where You will and deal with me freely in all things. I am in Your hand; turn me about whichever way You will. Behold, I am Your servant, ready to obey in all things. Not for myself do I desire to live, but for You—would that I could do this worthily and perfectly!"

PEACE BEYOND OUR UNDERSTANDING

Nurturing peace does not come naturally. Yet once you've discovered it, it seems like the only way that is natural or healthy. So live at peace with yourself. Live at peace with others. Live at peace with God. For peace is the best of all possible worlds. Yet you can only find it in this world if you are willing to glimpse into the next.

Work was hectic and responsibilities were heavy. Horatio Spafford had planned a lengthy vacation in Europe with his wife and three daughters, but there was too much to do. So he decided to stay in Chicago for a few weeks, send his family by ship to Europe, and join them as soon as he could. As his family traveled across the Atlantic, the ship ran into a terrible storm. As the crew tried to navigate the ship through the huge waves, it collided with another sailing vessel. Horatio's wife was rescued and taken to England, where she finally got a message to her husband: "Saved alone."

Horatio was shocked and grief-stricken. He took the next vessel to

England to be at his wife's side. As he passed over the place where his daughters drowned, the captain of the ship pointed to where the tragedy had happened. Horatio stared endlessly into the waves, silently praying for peace. Finally a smile crossed his lips as he scribbled the following words on a piece of paper:

When peace like a river attendeth my way,
When sorrows like sea billows roll;
Whatever my lot, thou hast taught me to say,
"It is well; it is well with my soul."

STEP ⑳

WATCH YOUR WORDS

Every day I am bombarded by thousands and thousands of words. There are newscasts, telephone calls, e-mails, music lyrics, conversations, movie and television dialogue, newspapers, books, radio, letters, billboards, and the list continues. Unless you're alone on a deserted island, you can't escape words.

Words are how we share our thoughts and feelings. They are the means by which we express who we are and reach out to others. Communication is the key to relationships, understanding, and growth. Words shape

- how we think;

- how we perceive the world;

- how others see us;

- how successful we will be;

- how peaceful we are;

- how we relate to others.

The great philosopher Ludwig Wittgenstein wrote, "The limits of my language are the limits of my mind." Words are incredibly powerful. The apostle James writes, "If we could control our tongues, we would be perfect and could also control ourselves in every other way. We can make a large horse go wherever we want by means of a small bit in its mouth. And a small rudder makes a huge ship turn wherever the pilot chooses to go, even though the winds are strong. In the same way, the tongue is a small thing that makes grand speeches. But a tiny spark can set a great forest on fire."[1]

Words are strong, but they are also fickle. They can help or hinder all within the same minute. Aldous Huxley wrote, "Thanks to words, we have been able to rise above the brutes; and thanks to words, we have often sunk to the level of demons." Words are a paradox. We can say such good words and such wicked words. James concludes his previous thoughts with: "So blessing and cursing come pouring out of the same mouth. Surely, my brothers and sisters, this is not right!"[2]

Too many of us don't think before we speak. We must consider our words carefully. Jesus warns us that "you must give an account on judgment day for every idle word you speak."[3] Therefore, we need to learn when to keep quiet. Here are twelve times when it's best not to speak:

① When we're in the heat of anger
② When we don't have all the facts
③ When someone else is talking
④ When we are tempted to joke about something serious
⑤ When we might be embarrassed by our words later
⑥ When our words might convey the wrong impression
⑦ When the issue is none of our business
⑧ When we are tempted to lie or distort the truth
⑨ When our words will damage someone's reputation
⑩ When our words might hurt a relationship
⑪ When we want revenge
⑫ When we have already said too much

Winston Churchill once said, "By swallowing evil words unsaid, no one has ever hurt their stomach." We can all think of times we wish we'd kept quiet. Yet once our words have come from our mouths, we can't take them back. And if we are not careful, our attempts to repair a situation can make it even worse. As a child I learned a song that said it well: "Be careful little mouth what you say." A sign in front of a church in Dubuque, Iowa, was even more direct: "Lord, please keep one hand on my shoulder and the other over my mouth."

NEGATIVE WORDS

Far away in the Solomon Islands is a village that practices a unique form of logging. If a tree is too large to be cut down with an ax, the villagers yell at it. A group of men creep up on a tree at dawn and scream at it as loud as they can. They do this for thirty days. Robert Fulghum writes about this in his entertaining book *All I Really Need to Know I Learned in Kindergarten.* He goes on to say that this yelling kills the spirit of the tree. At the end of the thirty days, the tree dies and falls over. Robert Fulghum insists that this is true, and his conclusion is: "Yelling at living things does tend to kill the spirit in them. Sticks and stones may break our bones, but words will break our hearts."

You can slaughter a person with your words. You can do harm that leaves scars for the rest of his life. Mother Teresa said, "Violence of the tongue is very real—sharper than any knife." Words can humiliate and injure deeply. One of my clients, Kathy, still remembers, thirty years later, how her third-grade classmates belittled her. Another client, Sam, cringes, forty years later, at how his father told him he would never amount to anything. Henry Wadsworth Longfellow wrote, "A torn jacket is soon mended; but hard words bruise the heart of a child." As a psychologist, I see daily how hard words can also bruise the heart of an adult. Words can close people down and take away their confidence. Words can do more damage than we ever thought possible.

Words are potentially dangerous. Therefore, as the apostle Paul warns us, "Do not let any unwholesome talk come out of your mouths."[4] Unfortunately, unwholesome words are far too common, even among people who are normally kind and caring. Yesterday, Stephanie sat in my office and wept. Stephanie is a bright, competent, loving mother of three teenage boys who leads a weekly woman's Bible study at her church. In between sobs, she told me that Cindie, one of her closest friends for ten years, had said that Stephanie had failed as a mother and that if she had had a deeper faith, her life would be better. Stephanie was shattered. "How could anyone be so mean?" she asked. I listened carefully and replied, "You are a great mom, but your kids aren't perfect. If that's what she expects, wait until her kids become teenagers. In terms of your faith, God knows that you seek him. I know her words hurt, but try not to let them drag you down." At that point I was reminded of Jean-Paul Sartre's saying: "Words are loaded pistols." Geoffrey Chaucer said it well too: "Keep well thy tongue and keep well thy friends."

Dangerous words come in all sorts of varieties. Some may sound meaningless and harmless, but they aren't. We must consider how they will be heard by others, not just what our intentions are. Dangerous words often take on a life of their own. The types of words I find most dangerous are

- cruel words

- confusing words

- dishonest words

- offensive words

- foolish words

- explosive words

- empty words

- divisive words

- insensitive words

- discouraging words

- abusive words

- arrogant words

People who use these types of dangerous words do great evil. Their pride or naïveté has turned their tongue into a brutal weapon. Through these dangerous words, trust can be betrayed, friendships broken, families divided, churches split, and communities fragmented. So please beware, for your tongue has an incredible capacity for damage.

POSITIVE WORDS

"May I speak to your manager?" asked Linda.

The twenty-year-old waitress at the local family restaurant looked a bit shaken but replied politely, "Yes, let me get him for you."

The manager appeared at the table a few minutes later and asked, "What can I do for you?" His professional distance told Linda that the manager was expecting another complaint from an unhappy customer.

"I just wanted to let you know," Linda began, "that our waitress was wonderful. She was friendly and had a great smile. When my kids couldn't make up their minds what they wanted, she waited patiently and asked them a few questions. After serving us, she double-checked to make sure we were all satisfied."

The manager was relieved, and the waitress was encouraged. As Linda left, the waitress squeezed her hand and said, "Your words made my day; thank you so much. People only talk to my manager when I blow it or if something is wrong."

Unfortunately, most of us are better at complaining than complimenting. If we only fully understood how powerful our words are! They can build bridges or break hearts; they can give hope or steal peace; they can be a glorious present or a deadly poison. Words can change a person's life. So let's do as Dan Nelson suggests when he says, "As soon as you see someone doing something good, tell him about it."

We all love praise. It encourages us and improves our attitude. Sam Deep and Lyle Sussman write in their book *What to Say to Get What You Want*, "Praise is perhaps the supreme interpersonal motivator." So I look for things to praise—effort, motive, accomplishment, attitude, words, and character. The apostle Paul says, "Let everything you say be good and helpful, so that your words will be an encouragement to those who hear them."[5] When I think back on those people whose words encouraged, motivated, and affirmed me, I smile. These are the people who helped me through difficult times and lifted me to success when I felt hopeless. Solomon wrote, "The words of the wise bring healing."[6] Louis Nizer reflects, "Words of comfort, skillfully administered, are the oldest therapy known to man."

We each can bring healing or harm. And often the failure to heal, when an opportunity avails itself, does damage. I challenge us all to pay attention to opportunities to speak healing. We should follow the example of Emily Dickinson when she wrote, "If I can stop one heart from breaking . . . if I can ease one life the aching, or cool one pain . . . I shall not live in vain."

Kind words are the best currency of good relationships. Cicero wrote, "The rule of friendship means . . . always using friendly and sincere words." Kind words are always uplifting. Neil Eskelin writes in *Leading with Love* that the five most powerful word combinations in the English language are

1. "Thank you."
2. "Would you, please?"
3. "What do you think?"
4. "I am proud of you."
5. "I love you."

With these words and others like them, I'm reminded of what Solomon says, "Wise words bring many benefits."[7] This is not an excuse for manipulation but rather a challenge for encouragement. Here are a few more powerful words and phrases:

- Great!

- That's right.

- You're doing fine.

- Fantastic!

- Keep it up.

- You can do it!

- Good job.

- I knew you could do it.

- Wonderful!

- Congratulations!

- Beautiful.

- You made my day.

- I'm impressed.

- I trust you.

- Outstanding.

- You mean a lot to me.

- Excellent!

- What a great personality.

These are just a few of the kind words you can share with friends, neighbors, and anyone you meet. Again Solomon has more wisdom on the subject: "Kind words are like honey—sweet to the soul and healthy for the body."[8] With a little effort, you will never run out of good things to say. I've come to the same conclusion as Goethe, the famous German playwright: "Be generous with kindly words."

Solomon was the wisest man in the world, and many of his collected proverbs are about watching your words. I have already referred to three of them in this chapter, but let me include seven more. Make sure that your words are

① **Helpful:** "The lips of the godly speak helpful words."
② **Encouraging:** "An encouraging word cheers a person up."
③ **Gentle:** "Gentle words are a tree of life."
④ **Right:** "It is wonderful to say the right thing at the right time!"
⑤ **Pure:** "The Lord . . . delights in pure words."
⑥ **Refreshing:** "Wise words are like deep waters; wisdom flows from the wise like a bubbling brook."
⑦ **Gracious:** "Whoever loves . . . gracious speech will have the king as a friend."[9]

Our use of words requires wisdom, responsibility, and grace. They lead to behavior, and that behavior impacts not only others but also ourselves. Frank Outlaw observed that "you should all watch your words; they become actions. Watch your actions; they become habits. Watch your habits; they become character. Watch your character; it becomes your destiny."

WRITTEN WORDS

I love getting letters, but I rarely send them. Ronald Reagan was a master at writing short letters. He wrote love notes to his wife, thank-you notes to those who had assisted him, and congratulatory notes to those he admired. Even as president of the United States, every morning he sat at his desk to write letters to those he knew and to many he had never met. Whether one agreed with his politics or his policies, Ronald Reagan was one of the most admired presidents of the twentieth century. He was called "the Great Communicator" because he knew the power of positive words, whether done in person, through speeches, or in writing.

Writing letters provides a great way to communicate thoughts and feelings so they are not forgotten. It also allows you to send a message when you can't connect with the person face-to-face. Fyodor Dostoyevsky, the Russian novelist, wrote, "Much unhappiness has come into the world because of . . . things left unsaid." Letters make sure things are not left unsaid.

In his wonderful little book written with his wife, Diane, entitled *The Letter Box*, Mark Button tells about the importance of letters. He encourages us to write for the future so our thoughts and emotions are not forgotten. He suggests we write to our children, grandchildren, spouse, friends, or any other meaningful person—letters that are not to be opened until some special occasion years from now. He writes letters for his children to read on their future wedding day, their fortieth birthday, and even on the day of his funeral. He wishes no positive thing to be left unsaid and no encouraging message to be lost.

Letters can promise magic moments for the future. During the Korean conflict my father was in the navy and stationed on the South Pacific island of Guam. Thousands of miles away from home, my twenty-year-old father was homesick and in love. For a year and a half he wrote to a young lady from a small town in Oregon. Finally he got the courage to write a letter asking her to marry him. My dad says it seemed like forever as he awaited a reply. When at last it arrived, he was ecstatic. Shortly after he returned to the States, my mother and father were married. Fifty years, six children, and eighteen grandchildren later, there are two faded and crumpled shoe boxes carefully stored on a shelf at my parents' home. These two boxes are stuffed full of Dad's priceless love letters.

When one can't communicate directly, letters can reach out with whatever message you wish. In *The Call to Love*, Linda Riley writes that a letter can

- express the weight of one's feelings;

- communicate that someone is missed;

- deliver the gift of encouragement;

- say someone noticed;

- display appreciation;

- heal hurts;

- bring resolution;

- build bridges;

- keep people connected;

- give comfort;

- provide honor and respect;

- show love.

As you can see, a letter can be very powerful. It speaks across space and time. It can communicate in written word what you might not be able to articulate verbally. Thomas Moore said it well: "Something happens to our thoughts and emotions when we put them into a letter; they are then not the same as spoken words. They are placed in a different, special context, and they speak at a different level."

Many years ago a poor boy was born with a terribly disfigured face. When women saw him, they screamed; when children encountered him, they cried in horror; and even when grown men caught a glimpse of him, they were unnerved. This boy would have been doomed if it had not been for his beautiful words. If people heard his voice without seeing his face, they were immediately drawn to his gentle, kind, and refreshing language. So he soon learned to cover his face with a mask and only use positive words. As he became a man, his words brought him great success. By his thirtieth birthday he had become the wealthiest, most respected man in the kingdom. He had married a lovely wife who had given him three beautiful children.

One day his wife, who had never seen his face, begged him to remove his mask. "But if I let you see my face," said her husband, "you will no longer love me." She insisted that this was not true. She even said that his failure to show his face was a sign that he neither trusted her nor loved her. For a year she persisted in her request. Finally, on a bright spring morning, with much trepidation, he took off his mask.

His wife gasped, and her husband quickly covered his face. "No!" she said. "Let me look again." Slowly he uncovered his face a second time. His wife sighed and placed a mirror before him. "Do you see?" she said. "Your face is the most handsome I have ever seen." As others in the kingdom saw his face they agreed, and many wondered how an ugly boy became such a handsome man.

Yet the man knew the secret. Beautiful words create a beautiful face. Therefore watch your words.

They have great power.

STEP ㉑

LEAVE A GREAT LEGACY

"I don't think we're going to get out of this thing," Todd Beamer told the Airfone operator. "I'm going to have to go out on faith."

And that is exactly what the thirty-two-year-old account manager from Cranbury, New Jersey, did. Todd left his home early in the morning, before his wife and two young boys were awake. He drove to the airport and boarded his flight for a quick business trip to California. Soon the world was shocked by the unfolding events of September 11, 2001. Two hijacked airliners collided into the twin towers of the World Trade Center, another plane crashed into the Pentagon, and a fourth plane was off-course and speeding toward Washington DC, with potential targets of the White House or the Capitol. This last plane was United Airline Flight 93—Todd Beamer's flight.

On board things looked grim. Three hijackers had control of the plane, and the passengers knew they were going to die. But Todd and two others were determined to do something about it. They had heard about the three other plane crashes and had decided to overpower the hijackers. "It's what we have to do," Todd said to the operator. He asked her to pray with him. Just before 10:00 AM, she heard him say, "Are you guys ready? Let's roll!"

Sounds of struggle and screaming, then silence.

The plane crashed in an empty field in rural Pennsylvania.

When Lisa Beamer was asked by reporters about her husband's heroism, she replied, "Some people live their whole lives, long lives, without having left anything behind. My sons will be told their whole lives that their father was a hero, that he saved lives. It's a great legacy for a father to leave his children." In another interview, Lisa said, "Todd lived every day trying to make little decisions that were in line with the big goals he had for his life."

Todd came from a family that believed in legacies. He had four loving Christian grandparents and two strong Christian parents who provided positive life examples. Todd's father, David, put it this way: "Passing the baton of faith was a priority in our home. . . . That's a legacy we didn't take lightly." Summing up Todd's actions on that blue-sky Tuesday morning, his father said, "The reason Todd acted with conviction and courage in those extraordinary moments when Flight 93 was falling to the ground was because he had maintained his integrity and values in the ordinary days of his life."

Life is fragile. You might live to be one hundred or you might die today. Last week a beautiful, sensitive, thirty-four-year-old woman was walking home from work when a car went out of control and hit her. The impact was so hard that her heart exploded, and she died instantly. No warning. No words. No time for anything. One moment all was well, the next moment she was gone. Randy Stonehill, a songwriter, said, "Celebrate each heartbeat because it just might be your last." Moses wrote, "Teach us to realize the brevity of life, so that we may grow in wisdom."[1] If you were to die today, what would be your legacy?

- What words would be remembered?

- What actions would be remembered?

- What personal qualities would be remembered?

- What achievements would be remembered?

- What social interactions would be remembered?

Everybody leaves behind a legacy of some sort when they die. To make sure that legacy is positive you must envision it, live it, and close it.

ENVISION YOUR LEGACY

More than a hundred years ago, the Swedish chemist and industrialist Alfred Nobel got a rare opportunity to see his own future.

Nobel was famous as the inventor of blasting caps, dynamite, and other explosives that became widely used in weapons and made Nobel quite wealthy. But that particular legacy came back to haunt him one day in 1888. Nobel's brother, Ludvig, had died while traveling in France. The local French newspaper got the information mixed up and reported Alfred's death instead. The headline of the obituary read: "The Merchant of Death Is Dead."

Alfred Nobel thus had the unusual experience of reading his own obituary while he still had time to do something about it. He was appalled to think that his life might be summed up with the phrase "merchant of death." So he envisioned something more positive and deliberately set out to change his legacy. In his will he dedicated most of his fortune to funding prizes for "those who, during the preceding year, shall have conferred the greatest benefit on mankind." These Nobel Prizes for physics, chemistry, medicine, literature, and peace—not the invention of dynamite—are what most people now associate with the name Alfred Nobel.

It would be wise for all of us to look at our lives and consider what kind of legacy we would leave if we died today. As we do this, it will help us to focus our priorities, clarify our purpose, make important changes, and live in the light of eternity.

Rick Warren writes in *The Purpose-Driven Life,* "God wants to use you to make a difference in this world. He wants to work through you. What matters is not the *duration* of your life, but the *donation* of it. Not *how long* you lived, but *how* you lived." Abraham Lincoln communicated the same thing when he wrote, "And in the end, it's not the years in your life that count. It's the life in the years." Fill your life with good. Set goals for yourself—mental, emotional, physical, relational, and spiritual goals. Stretch yourself to do what seems beyond your reach. Then seek God to make it possible. Robert Kennedy said, "Some men see things as they are and say 'Why?' I dream of things that never were and say 'Why not?'" I think we should all say "Why not?" a lot more than we do.

You were placed where you are with the resources and limitations you have for a reason. Martin Luther King Jr. said, "Set yourself earnestly to discover what you are made to do, and then give yourself passionately to the doing of it." Don't complain about what you don't have, but shape your legacy with what you do have. Formulate a personal mission statement and use it to shape your legacy. I have found there are four key aspects to any mission statement:

① **Make it clear:** easy enough for a twelve-year-old to understand.
② **Make it concise:** no more than two sentences long.
③ **Make it simple:** elementary enough to be recited by memory.
④ **Make it significant:** so important that it will make a true difference in your life and the world around you.

Before you formulate your personal mission statement, ask yourself: *What do I wish to pass on to future generations?* A positive legacy is a priceless gift to leave behind. It will transcend us and touch those we will never know and see. It will impact the future for either good or evil. As John Ruskin wrote, "When we build, let us think that we build forever. Let it not be for present delight. Not for the present only; let it be such work as our descendants will thank us." Therefore when you envision your own legacy, consider the following suggestions:

- You loved God.

- You made your marriage the best it could be.

- You took good care of your family.

- You were kind and generous.

- You were a true friend.

- You kept your word.

- You encouraged others.

- You had a great attitude.

- You helped those in need.

- You were a good role model.

- You forgave those who wronged you.

- You left this world a better place.

You might not be able to change your past, but you can certainly change the legacy you leave from this day forward. But you must be proactive. In J. R. R. Tolkien's classic, *The Fellowship of the Ring*, Gandalf says to Frodo, "All we have to decide is what to do with the time that is given to us." What Albert Nobel came to realize was that his day-to-day decisions affected not only the quality of his own life but the legacy he left for generations to come. He also realized that if you envision a new legacy and are determined to bring it to reality, it can happen.

LIVE A LEGACY

George Boldt was a humble man who worked at the front desk of a modest hotel. One evening an elderly couple came to ask for a place to stay.

"I'm so sorry," said George, "but all of our rooms are taken."

"But this is the last hotel in town," said the older man. "They are all full, and we are far from home."

George felt bad, so he offered them his own room. They hesitantly accepted.

The next morning the elderly man expressed his appreciation and said, "George, you're the kind of man who should be managing the best hotel in the country. Someday I'm going to build that hotel and let you manage it."

Several years later George received a letter from the elderly gentleman inviting him to New York City—enclosed was a round-trip ticket. When George arrived, his host took him to a large, fancy, newly constructed hotel in the heart of the city. "George, this is the hotel I built for you!"

George stared in disbelief at the Waldorf-Astoria Hotel. The elderly gentleman was William Waldorf Astor, one of the wealthiest men in America. George Boldt's compassion and faithfulness in a modest hotel was noticed. He had lived his legacy and was thus prepared to manage one of the most magnificent hotels in the world.

The truth is, we never know at what moment our life will become a legacy. That's why the decisions we make right now, both big and small, are so important. Therefore, consider carefully your words and actions. Jonathan Edwards wrote that the key to a positive legacy is "never to do anything which I should be afraid to do if it were the last hour of my life." In so doing, we live a life that outlasts us like a beautiful fragrance that lingers in a room long after the person has left. To switch metaphors, Wanda

Henderson wrote, "The seeds that we sow will continue to touch lives because the ripple effect of goodness is multiplied many times as the years go by." Our words and deeds are not as insignificant or stagnant as we believe; they live on in ways that are often beyond our imagination. As General Maximus says in the movie *Gladiator*: "What we do in this life echoes in eternity."

Each day is full of amazing opportunities to shape our legacy. Jesus said, "My purpose is to give life in all its fullness."[2] I want to embrace this fullness with an exuberance that influences those around me and how they approach their future. Amy Carmichael's motto was "Love to live; live to love." Mike Huckabee writes in *Living Beyond Your Legacy* that "the challenge of living beyond our lifetime begins with being more than a critic of what is wrong. We must strive to be a creator of what is right." Not only what is right, but what is healthy, loving, and dynamic. The apostle Paul tells his young coworker Titus to "live in this evil world with wisdom, righteousness, and devotion to God."[3] All of this assures that we are currently acting in such a way to build a worthwhile legacy.

Living rightly is not easy, nor does it come naturally. We all have our share of tests and trials and temptations. As we grow deeper and stronger, we gain wisdom. This wisdom enables us to stumble less frequently, and when we fall, to get up more quickly. Josiah Gilbert Holland, a nineteenth-century poet, wrote, "A time like this demands strong minds, great hearts, true faith and ready hands." Let me add that we also need consistent prayers. During a time of difficulty Paul prayed that "the way you live will always honor and please the Lord."[4] If we can do that, we are living our legacy. And that legacy will be good.

COMPLETE YOUR LEGACY

Benedict Arnold started with a great legacy. In 1775, at the age of thirty-three, he was an American patriot and friend of George Washington. For the next five years he served with distinction in one battle of the Revolutionary War after another. He was a brilliant strategist and a courageous soldier, who soon rose to the level of general in the Continental Army. He was an amazing man—intentional about his goals and bold in their execution. He rapidly became a true American hero, and Congress even acknowledged its "admiration of his gallant conduct."

Yet by 1780, General Arnold had grown bitter and self-absorbed. He became angry at not getting additional promotions, overwhelmed by heavy debt, and disgusted with congressional politics. So he developed a plan to seek revenge, get rich, and collapse the patriotic cause. He wrote a letter to the British army commander, promising to betray the American fort at West Point, New York, for a million dollars. His plans were discovered, and General Arnold escaped to join the British army. The following year he led several attacks against American forces, one of which burned down Richmond, Virginia.

Benedict Arnold did not leave a legacy as a hero but as a villain. His name has entered the English language as a synonym for "betrayer" and "traitor." Few Americans know how wonderfully he started. Benedict Arnold died in 1801, and his final words addressed how much he regretted destroying his legacy.

When you lose your way, you may very well lose your legacy. This reminds me of what Paul J. Meyer writes in *Unlocking Your Legacy*: "We will be remembered for what we actually do, not what we wish we had done." John Greenleaf Whittier put it this way: "For all the sad words of tongue or pen, the saddest were these: 'it might have been.'" Protect your legacy by completing your legacy. It's important to go the distance, ending well with your eye firmly on the goal.

I know far too many people who start well but fall before they finish. It's easy to get weary or distracted, but my mother taught me to not give up. She used to say, "Finish what you start," and I won't argue with my mother. The apostle Paul wrote, "So let's not get tired of doing what is good. At just the right time we will reap a harvest of blessing if we don't give up."[5] We all have been tempted to do what is comfortable or easy, rather than what is positive and right. John Maxwell writes, "Decision helps us start. Discipline helps us finish."

My Grandma Blanche left a wonderful legacy. She took aerobics classes until she was eighty-five, she taught a Sunday school class until she was eighty-six, and she prayed for me until she died at eighty-eight. On the day before she died, her pastor came to her house to comfort her, but Grandma Blanche was more concerned with encouraging him and praying for his needs. She lived a full life, even when her body failed her. Grandma Blanche was determined to not let anything stop her from loving God and loving people. Mark Twain said, "A man who lives fully is prepared to die at any time." And Grandma Blanche was well prepared. When Billy Graham was asked what surprised him the most about life, he responded with how fast the years pass. Therefore, make the most of them.

So how will you be remembered? George Orson Welles wrote, "I don't suppose I will be remembered for anything." How sad. On June 8, 1968, Edward Kennedy gave his brother's eulogy. He said he hoped that Robert would "be remembered simply as a good and decent man, who saw wrong and tried to right it, saw suffering and tried to heal it, saw war and tried to stop it." What powerful words. Your legacy needs to be envisioned, lived, and closed. At the end of his life, the apostle Paul wrote, "I have fought the good fight, I have finished the race, and I have remained faithful."[6] President Ronald Reagan once referred to these words when he spoke to a gathering in Washington DC: "If we trust in him, keep his word, and live our lives for his pleasure, he'll give us the power we need—the power to fight the good fight, to finish the race and to keep the faith."

What does it look like to finish the race? As I thought about that, I was reminded of an old story from the back hills of Arkansas. A young man was worn out from hiking all day deep in the woods. Suddenly the sky grew dark, lightning flashed, and rain poured from the heavens. The hiker searched for shelter, but soon his clothes were soaked to his skin. He was cold and wet and miserable. Then he saw a cabin. Rushing to it, he found it empty. No one was there, but on the front porch was a large stack of dry, seasoned wood. The hiker quickly built a fire in the fireplace. It burned warm and bright, and he was soon dry. Sitting back in a comfortable chair, he noticed a sign above the fireplace: "Enjoy this little cabin. Rest all you want, and stay as long as you wish. There is only one request, and that is that you leave the wood pile a little higher than you found it."

The goal is to leave this world a better place than you found it. Leaving a positive legacy is perhaps the most important thing we will ever do. Yet to effectively consider this, we must look beyond this life with all its successes and failures. Thomas à Kempis wrote, "It is vanity to focus only on your present life and not look ahead to your future life." My friend Randy

Alcorn calls this "living in the light of eternity." After all, Solomon tells us that "God has . . . planted eternity in the human heart."[7] We look into the night sky or examine the petals of a wildflower or the fingers of a newborn and catch a glimpse of eternity. If this current life is all there is, then we are the most pathetic of all creatures. But how is it possible to glimpse what does not exist?

The best legacies are lived with a focus on a reality beyond our current grasp. This stretches us. For faith "is the confidence that what we hope for will actually happen; it gives us assurance about things we cannot see."[8] It is a reminder that "this world is not our permanent home" and that we are, deep in our being, "looking forward to a home yet to come."[9] This life is simply a short layover on our way to an eternal home. C. S. Lewis wrote, "Hope . . . means a continual looking forward to the eternal world. . . . Aim at heaven and you get earth 'thrown in.' Aim at earth and you get neither." So let us aim at heaven as we live a life that is worthy here on earth.

God is watching and waiting. He is hoping that we will each leave a great legacy. In the last sentence of Solomon's existential treatise on life, Ecclesiastes, he writes, "God will judge us for everything we do, including every secret thing, whether good or bad."[10] This judgment involves an evaluation of our legacy, and based upon this evaluation the apostle Paul writes "that the Lord will reward each one of us for the good we do."[11] When this happens, I pray that a smile will cross God's lips, that he will place his hand on your shoulder and mine, and that he will say what Jesus said in the parable of the three servants: "Well done, my good and faithful servant."[12]

CONCLUSION
TRULY LIVE LIFE

"I think we live in an exciting age," said the president of a small college in Indiana, "an age of wonders and discoveries."

It was 1870, and the president was speaking to a group of pastors and church leaders. One of the young pastors asked, "What do you mean?"

"I believe the day is not far off when men will fly through the air like birds."

"Heresy," shouted the pastor. "The Bible tells us that the gift of flight is reserved for angels!"

These remarks were quickly forgotten as this pastor, Milton Wright, returned home to his family in Ohio. However, three decades later his two sons, Wilbur and Orville, made the first successful powered flight at Kitty Hawk, North Carolina.

Thankfully, Milton Wright's lack of vision did not discourage his sons. Jonathan Swift once said, "Vision is the art of seeing the invisible." But vision is more than just seeing. It carries with it the determination to turn "what might be" into reality. This is what the Wright brothers did when they ignited the dreams of a whole generation and took air travel from an impossibility to a way of life.

Vision directs us to an abundant life. These two brothers moved their vision into reality and showed the world what amazing things can take place when a vision is pursued. They shaped the future, for they realized that the future is full of possibilities.

Wisdom provides a road map for the future. It shows us the best route to get where we want to go. It also points out dead ends, danger zones, and impassable obstacles. Solomon wrote, "The prudent understand where they are going."[1]

Wisdom gives us vision. It provides hope for the future, for possibilities, for dreams, and for adventure.

We all need vision—it brings us joy and excitement and purpose. Bill Perkins writes in *Awaken the Leader Within*, "It's your dream of the future that will pull you out of bed in the morning."

With the map in our hand and our route plotted out, it's time to start our journey. And though we have made our plans, we must remember that God is ultimately in control. Solomon writes, "We can make our plans, but the Lord determines our steps."[2] Henry Van Dyke wrote: "Happy and strong and brave shall we be—able to endure all things, and do all things—if we believe that every day, every hour, every moment of our life is in God's hands." And his hands are good. He wants us to have a fantastic, satisfying life. Wisdom improves our life, and as we walk in wisdom amazing things will start to happen. As the prophet Isaiah wrote, "You will live in joy and peace. The mountains and hills will burst into song, and the trees of the field will clap their hands! Where once there were thorns, cypress trees will grow. Where nettles grew, myrtles will sprout up."[3]

Wisdom works! Starting today, step out with the confidence that God is in control and the determination that you will walk in his ways. The apostle Paul writes, "So be careful how you live. Don't live like fools, but like those who are wise."[4] Thomas Merton's strategy for wisdom is "Be good, keep . . . your eyes open, your heart at peace, and your soul in the joy of Christ."

A great life doesn't just happen. Wisdom must be lived out every day, every hour, every moment. In this book I have included twenty-one steps of wisdom. Choose some or maybe all of the principles I've presented here, and then figure out how you might apply them. Then go out and do them. As Elbert Hubbard wrote, "I believe there is something [worth] doing somewhere for every man ready to do it. I believe I'm ready, *right now.*" Jonathan Edwards was determined to truly live. He wrote: "I resolve to live with all my might, while I do live."

In the 1998 Academy Award–winning movie about World War II, *Saving Private Ryan*, Captain John Miller, played by Tom Hanks, leads eight men behind enemy lines to rescue the private, who has been singled out because his brothers have all died in the war and he is the lone surviving child in his family. The men complete their mission, but only with much loss of life. Toward the end of the movie Miller's last words to the private before he dies are, "Earn this."

Fifty years pass in a moment, and Private Ryan, now an old man, stands in a green meadow and stares at the white crosses of those who lost their lives to save him. He kneels before Captain Miller's grave and says, "Every day I think about what you said to me that day on the bridge. I've tried to live my life the best I could. I hope that was enough."

He stands up, and his wife comes to his side. With tears in his eyes, he says, "Tell me I've led a good life."

I don't know whether Private Ryan lived a good life or not. Yet this is the wish of every morally healthy person in this world. And I can assure you that if you earnestly apply the wisdom of these twenty-one steps, with God's help, you will live a good life—even a great life.

ENDNOTES

SEEK WISDOM
1 Proverbs 3:13-17, NIV
2 Proverbs 9:6, 12
3 James 1:5
4 Joshua 1:9

PAY ATTENTION
1 Proverbs 4:1, 20
2 Matthew 19:26;
   Philippians 4:13
3 Jeremiah 40:4
4 Genesis 28:16

LIVE INTENTIONALLY
1 Proverbs 4:25
2 Ephesians 5:17
3 John 10:10
4 Deuteronomy 31:6

KNOW YOURSELF
1 Psalm 139:14, NASB
2 2 Corinthians 12:10
3 Romans 12:6

KEEP BALANCED
1 Romans 12:2-3
2 Psalm 19:1-3; 48:9;
   77:11; 119:27, 48, 148
3 Philippians 4:8
4 Proverbs 3:13, 21
5 Hebrews 5:14
6 Psalm 26:2
7 Proverbs 27:19
8 Proverbs 4:23
9 Ephesians 1:18
10 Genesis 2:18
11 Ecclesiastes 4:10
12 Matthew 22:39
13 Psalm 90:12, NIV
14 See 2 Kings 6:15-17
15 Psalm 51:10, KJV

LET GO
1 Isaiah 43:18, NIV
2 Philippians 3:13-14

3 Proverbs 29:11
4 Psalm 37:8
5 Ephesians 4:31-32
6 Proverbs 12:25
7 See Matthew 6:25, 34
8 1 Peter 5:7
9 Matthew 6:19-21

REACH OUT
1 1 Peter 4:9
2 Romans 12:13
3 Hebrews 13:2
4 Romans 15:7, NIV
5 Proverbs 1:5, NIV
6 1 Thessalonians 5:11
7 2 Thessalonians 1:11
8 1 Corinthians 14:1

CELEBRATE
1 James 1:2
2 Habakkuk 3:17-18
3 Proverbs 17:22
4 Matthew 7:7
5 Proverbs 15:30
6 Romans 15:13, NIV

DIG DEEP
1 Proverbs 18:15
2 Proverbs 12:15; 13:20;
   19:20; 20:18

WORK HARD
1 Proverbs 13:4
2 Colossians 3:23
3 Proverbs 15:19; 21:25
4 Proverbs 12:1
5 James 1:4
6 Ecclesiastes 9:10

REST
1 Exodus 31:17
2 Isaiah 43:20
3 Psalm 23:2
4 Psalm 23:3

5 Isaiah 30:15
6 Psalm 131:2
7 Psalm 27:14
8 Psalm 46:10, NIV

CLING TO THE POSITIVES
1 2 Timothy 3:1-3
2 Philippians 4:8
3 Colossians 3:2
4 Galatians 6:7, NIV
5 Psalm 37:27
6 Ephesians 4:29
7 Psalm 118:24;
   John 10:10; 14:27;
   Matthew 19:26, NIV;
   Romans 8:31;
   Matthew 11:28;
   Romans 8:39;
   Matthew 28:20;
   Deuteronomy 31:6;
   Philippians 4:13
8 Psalm 136:1

DRAW CLOSE TO GOD
1 James 4:8
2 1 Chronicles 28:9
3 Jeremiah 29:13
4 Psalm 63:1
5 Genesis 28:16-17
6 Proverbs 1:7
7 Proverbs 14:27
8 Mark 12:30
9 Psalm 100:1-2
10 Proverbs 3:5
11 Psalm 32:8
12 1 Kings 18:21
13 Matthew 16:24
14 John 14:15
15 Matthew 22:39
16 James 2:22
17 Proverbs 3:9
18 Psalm 119:3
19 John 10:27

BUILD INTEGRITY
1 Proverbs 6:17-19
2 Proverbs 10:9
3 Proverbs 11:3
4 Psalm 34:14
5 Romans 12:9
6 Amos 5:14
7 Genesis 49:23-24

CULTIVATE COMMUNITY
1 Ephesians 4:32
2 1 Thessalonians 5:14
3 1 Thessalonians 4:18,
  2 Corinthians 1:4
4 Proverbs 17:17
5 Proverbs 27:6, NIV
6 Proverbs 27:17

BE COMMITTED
1 Revelation 3:15-16
2 Matthew 19:6, NIV
3 Psalm 127:3
4 Psalm 37:5
5 Romans 12:1
6 Matthew 16:24

LOOK FOR LESSONS
1 1 Samuel 16:7, NIV
2 Proverbs 30:25, 28
3 Esther 4:14, NIV
4 Isaiah 6:10
5 2 Corinthians 4:18, NIV
6 See Luke 8:43-48

ACCEPT MYSTERY
1 1 Corinthians 13:12
2 Isaiah 55:8-9
3 Colossians 1:17
4 1 Kings 8:27
5 Job 42:2

SHINE BRIGHTLY
1 Matthew 5:14-15
2 Proverbs 4:18

3 Genesis 1:2-4
4 Daniel 12:3
5 Proverbs 29:18, KJV
6 Psalm 30:5
7 1 John 1:5
8 Ephesians 5:8, NIV
9 Romans 12:9, NIV
10 Ephesians 1:18
11 Isaiah 40:31

NURTURE PEACE
1 Numbers 6:26
2 John 14:27
3 Colossians 3:15
4 Mark 10:43
5 Matthew 20:28
6 Luke 22:42, KJV
7 Philippians 4:7

WATCH YOUR WORDS
1 James 3:2-5
2 James 3:10
3 Matthew 12:36
4 Ephesians 4:29, NIV
5 Ephesians 4:29
6 Proverbs 12:18
7 Proverbs 12:14
8 Proverbs 16:24
9 Proverbs 10:32; 12:25;
  15:4; 15:23; 15:26;
  18:4; 22:11

LEAVE A GREAT LEGACY
1 Psalm 90:12
2 John 10:10
3 Titus 2:12
4 Colossians 1:10
5 Galatians 6:9
6 2 Timothy 4:7
7 Ecclesiastes 3:11
8 Hebrews 11:1
9 Hebrews 13:14
10 Ecclesiastes 12:14
11 Ephesians 6:8

12 Matthew 25:21

TRULY LIVE LIFE
1 Proverbs 14:8
2 Proverbs 16:9
3 Isaiah 55:12-13
4 Ephesians 5:15

SELECTED BIBLIOGRAPHY

Alcorn, Randy. *The Treasure Principle: Discovering the Secret of Joyful Giving.* Multnomah.

Augustine. *Confessions.* Fine Editions Press.

Baillie, John. *A Diary of Private Prayer.* Scribner.

Bauby, Jean-Dominique. *The Diving Bell and the Butterfly: A Memoir of Life in Death.* Vintage Books.

Beckett, Sister Wendy. *Meditation in Silence.* Dorling Kindersey Publishing.

Benner, David G. *Sacred Companions: The Gift of Spiritual Friendship & Direction.* InterVarsity Press.

Bickel, Bruce and Stan Jantz. *God Is In the Small Stuff . . . and It All Matters.* Promise Press.

Buchanan, Mark. *Your God Is Too Safe.* Multnomah.

Buechner, Frederick. *Now and Then: A Memoir of Vocation.* Harper and Row.

Carnegie, Dale. *How to Win Friends and Influence People.* Simon and Schuster.

Carter, Jimmy. *Why Not the Best?* University of Arkansas Press.

Chambers, Oswald. *My Utmost for His Highest.* Discovery House Publishers.

Chesterton, G. K. *Orthodoxy.* Doubleday.

Collins, Gary. *Christian Coaching.* NavPress.

Crabb, Larry. *Connecting.* Word.

Dillard, Annie. *Teaching a Stone to Talk.* Harper and Row.

Dobson, James. *Parenting Isn't for Cowards.* Word.

Eldredge, John. *Waking the Dead.* Nelson Books.

———. *Wild at Heart.* Nelson Books.

Eskelin, Neil. *Leading with Love.* Revell.

Foster, Richard. *Celebration of Discipline.* Harper and Row.

Frankl, Viktor E. *Man's Search for Meaning.* Pocket Books.

Giglio, Louie. *The Air I Breathe.* Multnomah.

Huckabee, Mike. *Living Beyond Your Lifetime: How to Be Intentional about the Legacy You Leave.* Broadman and Holman.

Julian of Norwich. *Revelations of Divine Love.* Penguin Classics.

Kadlecek, Jo. *Feast of Life: Spiritual Food for Balanced Living.* Baker Books.

Kelly, Thomas. *A Testament of Devotion.* Harper and Row.

Kempis, Thomas à. *The Imitation of Christ.* Ave Maria Press.

Lamott, Anne. *Traveling Mercies.* Anchor Books.

Lewis, C. S. *The Great Divorce.* Macmillan.

————. *Mere Christianity.* Macmillan.

Lindbergh, Anne Morrow. *Gift from the Sea.* Pantheon Books.

Mandino, Og. *A Better Way to Live.* Bantam Books.

Manning, Brennan. *The Signature of Jesus.* Multnomah.

Mehl, Ron. *Just in Case I Can't Be There.* Multnomah.

Merton, Thomas. *The Seven Story Mountain.* Harcourt Brace and Company.

Meyer, Paul J. *Unlocking Your Legacy: 25 Keys for Success.* Moody.

Nouwen, Henri. *Our Greatest Gift.* HarperSanFrancisco.

Packer, J. I. *Knowing God.* InterVarsity.

Parrott, Drs. Les and Leslie. *When Bad Things Happen to Good Marriages.* Harper Collins/Zondervan.

Peale, Norman Vincent. *The Power of Positive Thinking.* Fawcett Publications.

Peck, M. Scott. *The Road Less Traveled.* Simon and Schuster.

————. *The Different Drum.* Simon and Schuster.

Perkins, Bill. *Awaken the Leader Within.* Zondervan.

Powell, John. *Why Am I Afraid to Tell You Who I Am?* Argus Communications.

Riley, Linda. *The Call to Love.* Tyndale House.

Rowell, Edward. *Go the Distance: 21 Habits and Attitudes for Winning at Life.* Broadman and Holman.

Stanley, Andy. *The Best Question Ever.* Multnomah.

————. *The Next Generation Leader.* Multnomah.

Teresa of Avila. *The Interior Castle.* Riverhead Books.

Thoreau, Henry David. *Walden.* Peter Pauper Press.

Tournier, Paul. *To Understand Each Other*. John Knox Press.

Tozer, A. W. *The Pursuit of God*. Christian Publications.

Vanauken, Sheldon. *A Severe Mercy*. Harper and Row.

Vredevelt, Pam. *Letting Go of Worry and Anxiety*. Multnomah.

Warren, Rick. *The Purpose-Driven Life*. Zondervan.

Weber, Stu. *Locking Arms*. Multnomah.

Willard, Dallas. *The Divine Conspiracy*. HarperSanFrancisco.

Wright, Alan. *The God Moments Principle*. Multnomah.

Yancey, Phillip and Paul Brand. *Fearfully and Wonderfully Made*. Zondervan.

REMEMBER:

"*A book is . . .*
a garden, an orchard,
a storehouse, a party,
a company by the way,
a counselor, a multitude of counselors."

—HENRY WARD BEECHER